D1140224

tap here to
transform
your life

A PRACTICAL GUIDE TO
EFT

JUDY BYRNE

This edition published in the UK
in 2019 by Icon Books Ltd,
Omnibus Business Centre,
39–41 North Road,
London N7 9DP
email: info@iconbooks.com
www.iconbooks.com

First published in the UK
in 2014 by Icon Books

Sold in the UK, Europe and Asia
by Faber & Faber Ltd,
Bloomsbury House,
74–77 Great Russell Street,
London WC1B 3DA
or their agents

Distributed in South Africa
by Jonathan Ball,
Office B4, The District,
41 Sir Lowry Road,
Woodstock 7925

Distributed in Australia and
New Zealand
by Allen & Unwin Pty Ltd,
PO Box 8500,
83 Alexander Street,
Crows Nest,
NSW 2065

Distributed in Canada
by Publishers Group Canada,
76 Stafford Street, Unit 300
Toronto,
Ontario M6J 2S1

Distributed in the USA
by Publishers Group West,
1700 Fourth Street,
Berkeley, CA 94710

ISBN: 978-178578-468-2

Text copyright © 2014 Judy Byrne

Typeset in Avenir by Marie Doherty

Printed and bound in Great Britain by Clays Ltd, Elcograf S.p.A.

About the author

Judy Byrne is a therapist, trainer, author, speaker, and one of only 29 people worldwide to have been awarded the title of EFT Master by EFT founder, Gary Craig. She was privileged to do her own advanced training in a small group in the US with him. Her passion is to help people discover how they can be the way they want to be by getting the word out about EFT, so everyone can benefit from using it.

Judy has presented on EFT to large audiences worldwide and has been quoted extensively as an EFT expert in newspapers and magazines. She is on the executive board and is a trustee and chair of the ethics committee for EFT International (formerly AAMET International – the Association for the Advancement of Meridian Energy Techniques), the lead body for energy therapy standards worldwide. She has also devised and taught an approved hypnotherapy course, and taught on a psychotherapy course. She was a member of the National Council for Hypnotherapy and a fellow of the National Hypnotherapy society and had a private practice in London for more than 30 years before she moved to Queensland, Australia where she now lives.

Contents

Preface

This book is will explain how to use Emotional Freedom Techniques or EFT, an energy therapy that has swept the world over the last 25 years. Energy therapies combine working with the body's energy system and, at the same time, focussing on the emotion or symptom of the problem we want to change. EFT, for example, uses tapping on a sequence of nine points of the traditional Chinese meridian system, also used by acupuncturists, while saying words that help us to keep our attention on what it is we want tapping to change.

Google Emotional Freedom Techniques and you will find more than 300 million entries. But what is EFT?

The amazing popularity of the technique lies partly in its simplicity and partly in its complexity. It's simple to use – anyone can learn the tapping sequence that covers the points on the meridian system in a few minutes – yet it can be used to deal with complex issues. This book will first show you how to use these basic techniques, and then teach you to put it into practice at different levels and on different issues.

You will find this book easy to follow and its contents simple to work through, with a lot of guidance on how to do so. It will teach you how to use the technique on straightforward problems like a single negative emotion or physical symptom, and then it will move on to more complex issues such as anxiety, stress, insomnia, weight loss, stopping smoking, phobias, trauma, grief, improving performance and health and demolishing barriers to attracting abundance into our lives. Each of these topics has its own section or chapter, so you can either read the whole book through in order or, once you have the tapping basics under your belt, you can skip to the issue that is most relevant for you.

I will also show you how you can clear out all the old negative experiences that influence how you are in the world right now, as well as how to become your own therapist. EFT can disempower the after-effects of old trauma, whether it's big enough to be called officially trauma or is instead what we call 'small t trauma' or 'everyday trauma'. This is the less dramatic but cumulatively equally influential steady drip of negative experiences. EFT can help you to have a happier past, as well as a better future. It gives you a way to go back to these influential memories and, without in any way losing the memory, detach the negative emotions from it so we are no longer slaves to its effects.

EFT has a knack of showing you where you really need to go. You may start tapping on something small and suddenly find something more serious or more complicated has just jumped into your awareness. If that happens, keep tapping until the emotion has subsided or gone down to a manageable level.

It is important that you start working on small stuff; ideally small stuff that, as far as you know, is not linked to something more deep-seated. If you have major traumas in your past, particularly if they are early traumas, it may not be safe to work with them on your own. If you want to try, start with smaller stuff until you have made friends with EFT. And even then promise yourself that if you realize you're out of your depth alone, you will find help.

The ways in which therapy can make people's lives better has been a career-long fascination for me. Over the past few decades I have done a degree in psychology, two diplomas in psychotherapy, and one in clinical hypnosis. I've attended so many workshops I lost count years ago. I trained in Eye Movement Desensitization and Reprocessing (EMDR) and using Mindfulness in Psychotherapy. All of this has been immeasurably valuable. But I can honestly say that EFT has been the biggest single discovery of my professional life.

I have always sought ways of working that empower the people I work with, rather than make them therapy dependent. The ideal therapy, in my mind, is one that deals with trauma, but with the minimum risk of re-traumatization. In an ideal world, therapy also needs to work fast: if you're suffering, you want to be able to alleviate that as quickly as possible. EFT scores high on all three criteria. Of all the techniques I've learned in my career, it's the only one I use on myself. If I'm worried about something, I tap. If I'm left stressed by a demanding day, I tap. If I'm upset or hurt or angry I tap.

So I am delighted to be able to share with you this brilliant energy therapy technique so you, too, can use it for yourself. I hope you will find tapping really transforms your life. It has mine.

REMEMBER THIS!!! If you have major traumas in your past, particularly if they are early traumas, it may not be safe to work with them on your own. If you want to try, start with smaller stuff until you have made friends with EFT. And even then promise yourself that if you realize you're out of your depth alone, you will find help.

PART ONE
Introduction to EFT

---

1. What is EFT?

We live not only in the physical world, but also in a world of feelings and thoughts. Our inner world often seems more real than the one outside us and we often feel we have no control over either. But actually, our inner world is an inside job.

Some places make us feel anxious. Some people make us feel angry. Some memories make us feel sad. Some days just totally stress us out. But does it have to be that way? What if we could choose the inner landscape – the world of our thoughts and feelings and memories and hopes – that we live in? What if we had that power? What if we could totally control our anxious and angry and stressed responses?

What if you had a tool that enabled you to wind down when you are wound up, to let bygones really be bygones, to let you shrug off anger, face the future without fear or remember the past without bitterness or regret? What if you could learn a way to achieve inner peace?

Well, the good news is that there is a way. It's called Emotional Freedom Techniques, or EFT for short. If you're stressed or unhappy with your life or feel you are over-anxious or underachieving, or if you want your life to be different in any way, then use this book to give yourself some serious attention and you'll find you can have way more control over the state of your inner world than you ever imagined possible. And that comes with a built-in bonus. When we change how we feel it can change how others see us and treat us, which can change the way we feel even more, which can change how others see us – it's a virtuous circle.

 Not only can you use EFT to change how you feel in the moment but, with a little bit of time and attention, you can change your inner default setting. It's a whole lifestyle change, rather than a temporary fix.

EFT, or as you might have heard it called, 'tapping', is a paradox. Although it can be used in subtle, complex therapy, it can also be a deceptively simple self-help tool. That is true whether you're working with a therapist or doing it by yourself. You can use it to zap a current emotional or physical pain right now, or you can go back over negative things that have happened to you and change the way you live in the world.

Some people talk about EFT as being like emotional acupuncture. Others have described it as healing at 21st-century speed. It consists of tapping on the body at the meridian points – the ancient Chinese way of describing how energy is organized in our bodies – while putting our attention on exactly what it is that we want to change, and saying words that help us get and keep our attention focussed on what we are doing.

Tapping is a way of clearing emotions that are stuck in our systems. It draws on ancient Chinese wisdom in the same way as therapies like reflexology and acupuncture do, but it combines it with a very modern understanding of consciousness and psychology.

One of the best things about EFT is that it often shows us where we need to go. Even without any therapy skill it is likely that wherever you start, EFT will indicate to you what it is that you need to work on. It exposes connections we do not know consciously, and so cannot make for ourselves by logical deduction. It really does get to parts other therapy tools cannot reach.

In brief, EFT can help you to:

- Deal with negative emotions
- Banish or decrease physical symptoms
- Beat stress
- 'Rewrite' your past
- Allow you to be the person you want to be
- Help you to have the life you want to have
- Assist you to overcome self-imposed limitations
- Banish phobias
- Handle anxiety
- Help you stop smoking
- Change eating patterns
- Lose weight
- Make friends with your inner critic
- Improve performance

- Overcome insomnia
- Increase confidence
- Update your self-image

EFT is also really versatile. You can do it for ten minutes or an hour. You can find a quiet space and make an appointment with yourself to really invest time and attention in yourself – or you can do a quick few minutes in the lavatory to reduce your pre-presentation nerves if you find making presentations stressful. It will fit in with you.

 Jane found it really difficult to go in lifts. She couldn't work out what it was that made it so frightening. She knew if the lift broke down there would be an emergency phone, and at worst she might be stuck for a while but she would not be in danger. Yet she couldn't reason herself out of the deep terror she felt when she even thought about it.

She started tapping on all the EFT points on her body while putting her attention in turn on everything she could think of to do with this. She imagined she was waiting for a lift and tapped on the feelings that came up in her body just from thinking about it. She imagined being in it and tapped. She stood outside a lift and tapped on what she felt as she waited for it to open the door.

Then, she suddenly found her mind wandering. She started to think about a time when she was a little girl and shut herself in a cupboard when she was playing and was unable to open the door again. As she remembered it, she noticed the feelings that came up in her system were exactly the same as the ones that came up when she thought about going in a lift.

When she detached the emotion from that early memory, in the way you will learn in this book, lifts were no longer an ordeal for her. They were just the fastest way from one floor to another.

---

2. Where did EFT come from?

EFT's earliest roots lie in the tradition of Chinese acupuncture and the idea that energy is organized in the body around certain channels called meridians. There is reliable evidence that this concept has survived more than 5,000 years of use. Longevity does not, of course, prove anything but it does show that many hundreds of successive generations have found it useful.

We have indisputable evidence that it has been around at least as long as that. Rising temperatures in the Ötztal Alps between Germany and Italy caused a thaw which, in September 1991, revealed a well-preserved body. It was reliably dated to about 3,300BC. On it were tattoo marks for what would today still be the points an acupuncturist would use to treat arthritis and a stomach condition and the body showed that the man had had both.

Acupuncture has continued to flourish, and in the last 50 years a number of Western healthcare professionals became interested again in other implications of the meridian system. One of them was a chiropractor called George Goodhart, who founded Applied Kinesiology, a way of diagnosing physical conditions by the relationship between muscle strength and meridians. Another was the psychiatrist John Diamond, who brought emotions into Goodhart's ideas about physical diagnosis to found Behavioural Kinesiology, which used muscle strength in relation to meridians for emotional diagnosis and treatment. And a third was clinical psychologist Roger Callahan, founder of Thought Field Therapy (TFT), which was the direct predecessor of EFT.

In 1980, Callahan had a client called Mary with an intractable water phobia. She was so afraid of water that getting into a bath would bring on an anxiety attack. She could not bathe her children. She had nightmares about water. She was even afraid of rain. For two years he had tried all the conventional techniques. She could still only get as far as dangling her feet in a pool. And when she thought about water, she reported a strong sensation of fear in her stomach.

When she told Callahan where she felt the fear, he did an experiment. He tested his knowledge of meridians by tapping a point associated with stomach sensations. He thought it might help the discomfort in her stomach. He was amazed when she suddenly said the phobia had disappeared. (Not only did she say she no longer felt afraid of water but, to Callahan's dismay, she began running enthusiastically towards the swimming pool. He knew she could not swim.)

He began experimenting to see which points needed to be tapped to clear which specific emotions and developed a series of protocols to deal with them. As his knowledge base increased, he started teaching other therapists with an appetite for exploring the unconventional.

One of the people who did Callahan's TFT training in the early 1990s was a Californian personal development coach called Gary Craig. Craig had an engineering degree from Stanford, and though he had never actually worked as an engineer he had an engineer's mindset when he reflected on what he had learned on the course.

He came up with the idea that the series of specific tapping protocols of TFT could be simplified into a single sequence that covered all bases. Admittedly, it would be a longer sequence and have some redundancy built in. For each person who used it some points would not be relevant, at least for the problem they were dealing with. But it would, he reasoned, be quicker to do them all than to spend time working out which ones to use when. It would also leave plenty of attention available for what was being tapped on, as opposed to worrying about where to tap.

When you use it yourself you will find that the sequence quickly becomes so automatic that you will do it without even thinking about where the points are. This leaves your full attention for concentrating on what it is you want to deal with. That is just as it should be.

REMEMBER THIS!!! It is key when you are tapping around the meridian points and repeating the words you have chosen to say, that you keep all your attention on what it is you are tapping on – what you feel and where and how you feel it. The entire point of the words is to help you to keep your attention focussed.

---

3. What can EFT do for me?

The purpose of EFT is to give us power over our thoughts, feelings and emotional state. It enables us to change the life we are having to the life we want. It is a portable tool that we can use quietly and privately by ourselves, or that we can take with us into situations that cause us problems. We always have it literally at our fingertips.

The thinking behind EFT is this: stuff happens. That stuff might be a negative or even traumatic experience, or a negative thought pattern, or a destructive relationship. The result is disruption of the body's energy system. Even if you are sceptical about the ancient Chinese vision of the body's energy system, you will have felt how stress or trauma can have a physical effect. Stress can give you a pounding headache, or a sudden shock can leave you feeling your legs are going to buckle under you. EFT can help us by soothing the energy system disruption when we tap on certain points, while putting our attention on the negative emotional and physiological feeling that we want to rid ourselves of.

So what EFT can do for you can be really simple – like getting rid of anger from a row five minutes ago, or making a lifelong phobia go up in a puff of smoke. Or it can be subtle and complex – like clearing the residue in our systems from years of negative childhood experiences in which we were constantly criticized or discouraged or hurt, for example.

TRY IT NOW! Write down the earliest negative memory you have. For example, your mother going out and leaving you with someone you did not really know well. When you think about it, how high, on a scale of 1–10, would you rate the negative emotion attached to it <u>at this moment</u>? Now, try to get a sense of what impact it would have had when it happened. Imagine you're back at that age again and see if you can what impact on a scale of 1–10 it had on you <u>then</u>.

Keep this in mind whenever you are deciding what is worth spending time focussing on. The impact of an experience is not what it would be if it happened at your current age but what it was when you were the age at which it happened.

Identifying what to work on

We human beings operate by template matching. At any minute there is far more information available to us than we could possibly process. In your present surroundings there will be more sights and sounds and smells and tastes and sensations than any human brain could possibly perceive, so we need to have a way of choosing what we notice and what just passes us by.

We do this by matching up what is present with what is past. The experiences and relationships we have had influence first what we are actually aware of in any situation and then whether we react to it as safe, unsafe or neutral.

For example, if you have been mugged walking down a street in the dark, next time you are walking down that street and hear footsteps behind you, you might be more inclined to feel really anxious. Or you might find yourself 'predicting' the behaviour of a new partner based on your experience of your last relationship.

Template matching enables us to function in a world of information overload, without blowing a neural fuse or just shutting down in the face of so much stimulation. But it also means that we automatically judge every situation we encounter by whether, when we had a similar experience before, it was good, bad or neutral. It happens out of conscious awareness and so fast that we do not even catch it, let alone have time to argue with it. Subconsciously, we are trapped by the patterns of the past.

 Not only does what has happened to us determine how safe we feel the world to be but also who and how we are in it. Break those patterns, and you are free to be who you want to be.

EFT can disempower the after-effects of old trauma, whether it's big enough to be called trauma or is what we call 'small t trauma' or 'everyday trauma'. This is the less dramatic but cumulatively just as influential steady drip of negative experiences.

EFT can help you to have a happier past, as well as a better future. It gives you a way to go back to these influential memories and, without in any way losing the memory, detach the negative emotions from it so we are no longer slaves to its effects. It can be truly transformative.

4. How do you do EFT?

Much of this book will be the long answer to that question. But to get started, here are the absolute basics:

1. Decide what negative emotion you want to work on.

2. Rate its intensity on a scale of 1–10. How much does it distress or disturb you? This is called SUDS, short for 'subjective units of distress/disturbance scale'.

3. On the side of the hand point (see diagram on the next page), you tap firmly with the tips of three fingers while you say this set-up statement three times: 'Even though I have this (describe the problem feeling here) I accept myself.'

Self-acceptance is key to successful EFT as it is to many different therapies. It is also a key component of Mindfulness. It is a way of acknowledging that, although a part of you has the problem you just described, you're okay with yourself, in spite of it. You can, if you prefer, say: 'I accept myself', or 'I deeply and completely accept myself', or 'I accept myself anyway.'

I'm now going to do a run-down of each tapping point in detail. When you tap on a feeling, you should go round these points in turn.

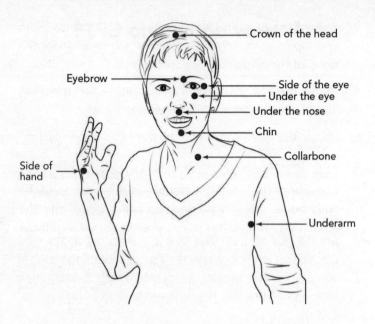

Crown of the head

Eyebrow

Side of the eye

Under the eye

Under the nose

Chin

Collarbone

Side of hand

Underarm

1. **Crown of the head.** Make your fingers into a bunch and tap with the tips of all five fingers around this point. Half of the meridians in the body meet here, so it is a particularly powerful point. The Chinese name for it translates as a metaphor that means 'the meeting of a thousand pathways'.

2. **Eyebrow.** This is on the nose end of the eyebrow, straight above the tear duct. It's easiest to tap with the tips of two fingers here because you cover a big enough area so that if you are a bit out, you are still hitting the spot.

3. **Side of the eye.** This is still on the eye socket, so when you tap it – two fingertips again – you should feel the bone of the socket under your fingers.

4. **Under the eye.** You are still on the socket, so, as before, feel the bone and use two fingers.

5. **Under the nose.** On the fleshy part above the top lip.

6. **Chin.** Between the bottom lip and the point of the chin.

7. **Collarbone.** This point is actually at the junction of the collarbone, the first rib and the breastbone, and the easiest way to find it is to run your fingers along under the collarbone until you feel it meet up with the rib and breastbone, in a slightly off-centre little dip. If you are really having trouble finding this and using two fingers, you can thump with your fist about where a man would knot his tie.

8. **Underarm.** This is about nipple level and depending on the person can feel somewhere between slightly sensitive and painful. If you have trouble finding it, imagine you are zipped up the side and the point is on the top of the zip. Tap firmly with two or three fingers.

As you work through the book, you may find a particular point is especially powerful for you. If you do, you may want to use it more often or for longer than the other points. You might even experiment with using it on its own at times.

Here is a simple exercise to start.

1. What are you feeling right now that you want to free yourself from? Is it anxiety? Or anger? Or sadness? Or a headache? When you have decided, take note of where and how you feel it in your body. What you feel in both senses – the emotional and the physical – is important in EFT. Marrying the two helps maximize the effect.

2. How high, on a scale of 1–10, would you rate the intensity of your feeling?

3. How would you describe these feelings to yourself? The words, in a sense, do not matter. They are not a magic mantra. The importance of describing accurately and in detail is because it's key that you put your attention, as closely as you can, on *what* you're feeling. Formulating a detailed description is a good way to do that. So it might be something like: 'This dull, heavy anger in the pit of my stomach …', or 'this burning knife of anger in my chest …', or 'this burning red ball of anger in the middle of my chest'.

4. Access on a scale of 1–10 how intense your bad feeling is, where ten is the worst you can imagine and one is hard to notice at all. If you feel you really cannot put a number on it, then guess. Guessing will access what you know unconsciously.

5. Now tap around the meridian points shown in the earlier diagram. Tap firmly, as if you mean it, but not hard enough to give yourself a headache or to feel discomfort.

6. Start on the side of the hand point and say three times: 'Even though I have this (dull, heavy anger in the pit of my stomach, for example), I deeply and completely accept myself.' Say it three times. Try as much as you can to keep your attention on the feelings you are describing.

7. Now take a reminder phrase from that statement. In the example above, it would be: 'This dull heavy anger in the pit of my stomach …'. Repeat it a couple of times as you tap on each of the other points in the picture. Start at the top of the head and end with the underarm point. Tap around that sequence, from the top of the head to under your arm, a second time, still repeating the reminder phrase.

8. Decide where you are on the scale again.

9. Has the number gone down? Let's say you started at an eight and it's now a five – you can either do another round of all the points in the sequence, just varying it by saying, 'Even though I still have some of this dull, heavy anger in my stomach,' and the reminder phrase, 'remaining dull, heavy anger in my stomach'. Or, if the feeling or its location has changed you can reword

it completely. So it might now be something like, 'Even though I have this grey lump of irritation in my throat …'. Each time it changes, chase it down with your words and your attention until it's gone.

 Tell it like it is. When you're deciding what words to use, use the language that you would use in your head, if no-one else was listening in. If you feel like swearing about it, swear about it. If you do a polite, cleaned up version, your unconscious mind will not really get what it is that you're talking about. The key to successful EFT is being honest with yourself.

---

5. Working with bad memories

There is a saying in EFT about 'the writing on your walls'. The 'writing' refers to the beliefs we have, both those we know we have and those controlling us from below the level of our awareness. They tell us who we are and how we feel about ourselves, and how safe, or otherwise, the world is. These beliefs come from what we learned from parents, caregivers, teachers, playmates and many other sources. They come from classmates and friends. They come from the experiences we did not have as well as the ones we did.

Think about it this way: does a baby who cries and cries and no-one comes think, 'This is unsatisfactory parenting'? Or does it think, 'I need stuff and I don't know how to get it'? Or 'I need stuff and I cannot be sure I will ever get it'? Or even, 'The world does not care about me. I must be bad or unwanted or unloved or unlovable'? Of course, no baby could articulate these questions in those words. But even a young baby can begin to feel them. Beliefs like these can start to build up from very early on.

Fast-forward a few years. The child comes home from school and rushes into the kitchen to tell his mother, 'I got 98 on my test today.' And the mother says, 'What happened to the other two marks?' So he works harder and next time he comes home and says, 'I got 100 per cent.' And this time his mother says, 'How many others in the class got 100 per cent?'

Maybe he still does not actually put it into words, but there could be some major life-defining writing coming up again here. It could be: 'No matter how hard I try it's never good enough, so I'll just give up trying.' Or it could be: 'I have to keep trying and trying and trying and …'. Here in the making, potentially, is either someone who drops out and stops trying at all, or a perfectionist who cannot hand in a report or an assignment in case it is not yet good enough.

We tend to mistake these beliefs about ourselves and the world for truth, whether they are true or not, whether we have evidence for them or not, and whether they serve us well or badly. One of EFT's great strengths is that it gives us a tool to challenge the emotions and the beliefs stored in our systems, initially derived from all those early experiences and which we constantly top up for ourselves by our current experience – who we hang out with, what we watch on television, what we read, what we listen to.

What is a negative memory?

- **A negative memory** is anything that is stored in our heads as having been a negative experience, whether or not we still feel emotion about it. If it had been neutral, it would almost certainly be forgotten now.

- **A negative memory** is rarely an accurate historical recollection of what actually happened. Every time we remember something we edit it in some way, and what we put back into storage is never exactly what we retrieved. Memory is constructed, rather than fixed; it is an edited and re-edited recording, rather than the original one.

- **A negative memory** is a negative memory whether we actually really remember it or not. You know those family stories you hear about yourself so many times that in the end you really do not know if you do remember it or you have just stored a version you imagined from hearing about it? That can still count. It's what is in your head that matters.

- **A negative memory** can be something that did not even happen to you. Sometimes we imagine things that we hear about or see on television so vividly that it gets to be stored in our head almost as if it was our own experience. And it can have just as much influence on us.

- **A negative memory** is sometimes a composite. If something happened over and over, especially when we were children, we might find it hard to know what is an actual historic negative memory and what is a composite of a number of them. But it really does not matter. What counts is what we have stored in our heads, not what actually happened.

 Write down three early negative memories. It doesn't matter how small they seem now. This is because we only remember the highs and the lows, so if you remember it, it mattered at the time. Also, even if it seems to be no big deal to you at the age you are now, just try to imagine what it felt like when you were the age you were when that happened.

This will give you a more accurate idea of how influential it has been. What gets to be 'written on our walls' reflects the emotional charge something had at the time, not our revision of it years later.

Keep a note of these memories. We will be coming back to them soon.

 Marianne had a phobia of water. Together we worked on a number of different past experiences that involved water and that she recalled with distaste. But they didn't really seem to have had the emotional intensity that might account for a phobia. And, though the symptoms were reducing, they did not clear. I was convinced that there had to be a missing piece of the jigsaw.

I remembered her mentioning that her mother had nearly drowned long before she was born. Obviously she couldn't have seen it, but when I asked her if she had a picture of it in her head she began to describe in vivid detail how her mother's long hair was caught up in the reeds, how her mother was struggling …

She had made a complete inner imaginary film of the event. Once we processed that 'false' memory as if it was a real one, the phobia passed into history.

Can EFT erase memories?

No, not in the sense of making you forget that it happened. Would you want to? That would be really unhealthy. Without our memories we would lose all sense of who we are, and we would go on making the same mistakes over and over. Our 'story' is what gives us a sense of ourselves. But what EFT *can* do is to detach the negative emotions from where they are stored, and hence eliminate the emotional aftermath. And once we are no longer emotionally attached to the memory, we often spontaneously discard or change the belief that it gave rise to.

How can I zap the emotions of a negative memory?

The following technique works on memories or snippets of memories that are short, and that have only one high point of emotion. If the memory you want to debug is long and/or has one or more emotional peak you will need to break it down into shorter episodes. You might want to try this out on one of the memories you wrote down earlier, as long as it is not something of really high emotional intensity. It will be more useful for you to start fairly gently – it might be something like hearing a classmate you thought was a friend saying something really nasty about you to another classmate when you were in the gym at school.

So if the three early memories you recalled are all big ones, or you know or suspect they connect to something big, go for a recent event of lower intensity but which left you feeling angry or upset or disappointed or uncomfortable. It might, for example, be something someone said to you. Or something you said and just wanted to bite your tongue the second it was out of your mouth.

The Movie Technique

This is one of EFT's best workhorses and you will use it over and over in your EFT journey.

It is amazingly simple, and suitable for working on issues of all levels of emotional intensity. When you have chosen a short memory that fits the description above, imagine you have it on a DVD on your memory shelf. (This is not an ideal metaphor in some ways because memory is not really a static recording like a DVD, but it is useful in this context.)

Give your DVD a title. What are you going to call it to distinguish it from the other DVDs in your memory collection? Let's say you're going to call it *OMG did I really say that?* See how high the emotion goes when you run it in your head now. Remember that for this exercise it's the emotion you feel *now*, not the emotion you recall at the time it happened, that you're trying to access.

Tap on the side of the hand point while you say three times, 'Even though I have this *OMG did I really say that?* memory, I deeply and completely accept myself.' Now tap round the points, twice, from the crown of the head to the underarm point, saying the phrase, 'This *OMG did I really say that?* memory'.

When you finish the second round of tapping, run the memory in your head again. How high does the emotion go now? Let's say it was six and has gone down to three. You can repeat it with a new set-up – 'Even though I still have some of this *OMG did I really say that?* memory …' and the reminder phrase round the points: 'Remaining *OMG did I really say that?* memory.'

Again check how much intensity is left, on the 1–10 scale. Repeat until your emotions are at zero.

What do I do now?

If you found yourself laughing or just feeling indifferent about the memory you are probably done.

If the memory is not yet zero, you could do another round of tapping, or you could try telling yourself the story. If you're in a situation where you can, tell it out loud. Otherwise, tell yourself silently. As it unfolds, notice if you feel even the tiniest bit of emotion. If you do, stop and tap it away. Then carry on. When you can tell the story start to finish without feeling any emotion you are done.

Other chapters will look at how we deal with more deeply traumatic memories, and at how to become your own therapist by working on your Personal Peace Plan (which we will explore in the next chapter). It is an excellent way to deal with the negative memories from which your default setting is derived. Change the emotions from the old memories and your default settings will change.

 It is really important to use your first language, especially when you are dealing with things that happened early in your life. If you speak your second language excellently and even think in it, then it is optional which language you use to tap on a recent event. But for early experiences, first language wins every time.

---

6. Being your own therapist: Your Personal Peace Plan

ETT gives you a way to become your own therapist. If you want to work on a specific problem, such as stopping smoking or coping with panic attacks, you can first go to the chapter in this book specific to your problem and work through it. Or, you can first work through the Personal Peace Plan in this chapter to eradicate the roots of anything that is troubling you, or you can do both. It's your choice.

You will also find the Peace Plan useful if you cannot pin down quite what you want to change. If, for example, you cannot put your finger on anything in particular that is wrong but just feel your life lacks sparkle, or contentment, or zest.

The Personal Peace Plan was devised by EFT creator Gary Craig and is simply this: you make a list of all your negative memories, and then you work through them, using the techniques for dealing with negative memories described in this book. Each time you are tapping on one memory and another pops up, add it to the list. Each time you clear one, cross it off.

It means you don't need to work out exactly what underlies your problem. When you have dealt with the events that gave rise to each negative issue they will just pass into history rather than running your present life the way they do now.

REMEMBER THIS!!! Some memories are really too big to deal with safely on your own. If you have a history of early abuse, or if you have been sexually assaulted, or you know you have post-traumatic stress, for example, you might need to have support to work safely.

If you do decide to try to go it alone, at least promise yourself that if you find you are out of your depth you will get help. (Sources are provided at the back of this book.)

So which memories qualify?

Everything you remember as having been negative at the time is a negative memory. It does not matter if now, when you run it in your head, no emotion comes up. If it had not mattered you would not still remember it as having been negative.

What we need to access in order to work on memories with EFT is the level of emotion we have when we run them in our heads now, or, if we know that it would still be really high, what we guess it would go to if we did run them, as in the Movie Technique. We are not trying to recapture what the level of emotion was at the time it happened.

Ironically, if the emotion is zero on the 1–10 scale, you may find that when you start tapping you start to feel worse. If you get more of the emotion back it probably means that you had repressed the feeling and tapping has lifted the repression. But if you still cannot access the feeling, tap anyway. You will need to go by other indicators, such as whether the memory seems still to be stored in the same way.

Has it faded? Does it seem longer ago or further away? Has the volume turned down? Has it gone from clear to fuzzy? These are all indicators.

How do I work on each memory?

You go through each one using the Movie Technique, described earlier, or the Tearless Trauma Technique, which is a variation on the Movie Technique where if the emotional intensity in going to be high you guess at where you would be on the scale without running the DVD in your head. Both of these techniques are revisited in the appendices at the end of the book.

What if I am scared to start working on a particular memory?

It depends. Is this something your common sense tells you that you shouldn't be working on on your own, as in the warning above? If it is, follow your instinct and don't do it alone.

But if it is something you feel you could deal with but would be anxious about doing it with or without help, then sneak up on it. You can tap on exactly what you are feeling about doing it before you do. Something like, 'Even though I'm afraid to start this, I deeply and completely accept myself …', or 'Even though this scares the hell out of me …', or 'Even though I have this heavy deep dread in the pit of my stomach when I think about starting this …'.

What order should I work on my memories in?

You can approach your memories in any way that makes sense to you. Some people do them in age clusters. What do you remember from each year of your life? Or each decade? Other people like to cluster them according to who else was in them. So maybe mother memories, father memories, brother memories, sister memories, school memories, and so on. Some go for clustering memories that they feel contributed to the same feelings about themselves – events they remember sapping their confidence in themselves or giving them a low opinion of themselves.

Some people just like to put things down in the order they come into their heads when they sit in front of a blank page and start writing. And there are some who like to start with what they think is worst and go from there. But a warning, here. If this is your first introduction to EFT, ease yourself in a bit more gently than that. Go for something bad, if you want to, but not the worst. Otherwise, do what makes sense to you.

Should I keep a record?

It is really good to keep a record. It will help you see that you are making progress, and it will help you make connections between events or issues. It will remind you of things that came up while you were tapping on another memory and put aside to work on later.

It is also good to make it a fairly solid physical record – a book or notepad rather than scraps of paper. Maybe even treat yourself to a really attractive book or folder. It gives you the message that you're really, seriously, going to work on this. That you are really worth it.

Should I do it at a set time?

If you're organized enough and can set the time for each session then that's great. But in the real world that might just be an impossible dream. You may have to settle for seizing the chance if you find yourself with a spare hour, if you keep promising yourself a particular time slot and then finding life gets in the way and it has to go on hold.

Still, it's good to try to actually make an appointment with yourself and keep it. After all, if you were paying to go to a therapist you could not just turn up at her office when you had an hour to spare. You would have to book in advance.

 When could you schedule some regular time to practice EFT? Maybe each weekend you could even go through your diary and book in some time to do it? Put some time in your diary now. It does not matter how long or how much. In an ideal world you might want to put aside half an hour to an hour most days while you do this project. But who lives in an ideal world? The only essential is that you keep records so you can pick up next time.

What if memories keep troubling me at the end of a session?

When you finish the session, close your eyes if you visualize better that way. Imagine you are somewhere you feel safe. Now imagine that you can see a vault – a bit like a night safe at a bank. You can put things in but no-one, including you, can get them out the same way. You need a combination for the lock. And the combination is what you decide it will be.

Now, imagine yourself putting all the DVDs that carry the memories you have not yet worked on into the vault. They will stay there until you decide that you are ready to start work again. Until then, no-one will have access to them. And don't forget to write the combination down in your Personal Peace Plan book.

If you start with a list of 100 memories and work through one a day, it will only take you three months to clear them all.

---

7. Making friends with your inner critic

Most of us live on intimate terms with our inner critic. Our inner critic is the part of ourselves that tells us, 'Those people probably won't like you', or 'You'll never manage to do that, so don't even try', or 'They'll judge you', or 'If you say something everyone will look at you', or even 'Nobody could love you.'

Some of us hear our inner critic as a voice. Others experience it as a thought. For still others it's a gut feeling that does not have words but is just as powerful. If you don't think this applies to you, then ask yourself two questions. First, do you keep yourself so busy that you make sure you never have time to hear the negative voice? And, if the answer to that is 'no', then ask yourself, do you hear it but mistake what it is saying for the truth?

The inner critic is, of course, a part of ourselves. And it is on a mission. Unlikely as this may sound, its mission is to do something positive for us – even if its effect is actually to do the exact opposite. So an inner critic that says 'Those people probably won't like you' might be trying to spare us the humiliation or the disappointment of being rejected. Or it might say, 'Don't even try' to protect us from the disappointment of failing. Or it might say, 'Don't say anything or they will judge you' to rescue us from our anxiety around groups of people or people we do not know well.

In other words our inner critic may feel as if it just picks on us and limits us and makes sure we are never at ease in the world, but its whole purpose in our life may be to try to make life easier/safer/less anxious for us.

How can tapping help?

Tapping is, first of all, a good way to acknowledge that we really do understand what this critical voice or thought or feeling is about. It is a good way to let the part of us that runs it know that we appreciate its intention but to ask it to change. As you continue to tap, you can ask it to try to help you in a different way.

We often have a situation where one part of us wants one thing and another wants something different, or some-times even the absolute opposite. But, as far as we can, it's better to resolve these internal conflicts and have all the different parts of us working together, on the same team. When we tap in the way outlined below, we are tapping on our energy systems and talking to the unconscious mind – the part of us that is not in our conscious awareness – as well as to our conscious mind.

Tapping with your inner critic
We're going to work through a full EFT cycle to recruit the help of your inner critic now. Use

42

these words or change them to what resonates with you and fits your experience. The more you let the ideas here guide you but tailor the actual words to you and your own real experience, the more powerful it will be for you.

Remember, the set-up statement you use on your side of the hand and the reminder phrase you use as you tap around the points have to be the words that describe what you feel in as much detail and as accurately as you can.

Tap on the **side of the hand** point and say something like: 'Even though I have this voice (or thought or feeling) that tells me I'm not good enough, I deeply and completely accept myself.' Then: 'Even though I have this part of me that is always telling me I am not good enough, I accept myself anyway.' And then: 'Even though it tells me all the time, I appreciate its intention. I thank it for trying to help me in its way, and I accept myself without judgement.' Then tap around the points from the top of the head to under the arm as follows:

Crown of the head: 'I thank this part of me for what it is trying to do for me.'

Eyebrow: 'I know it is on my side.'

Side of the eye: 'I thank it for that.'

Under the eye: 'I really appreciate it.'

Under the nose: 'I am grateful.'

Chin: 'I know it wants to help.'

Collarbone: 'I am really grateful.'

Underarm: 'I want to say thanks.'

Crown of head: 'I really want this part of me to stay part of me.'

Eyebrow: 'I want it to be part of me.'

Side of the eye: 'But I need this part of me to know this is just not working.'

Under the eye: 'I know it means well but this is just really negative for me.'

Under the nose: 'It is making my life really difficult.'

Chin: 'I just want to ask it to find a different way to help me.'

Collarbone: 'I want it to be really creative.'

Underarm: 'I am asking it to do things in a different way'

Learning from your inner critic

Your inner critic may be failing to help you in the way that it intends, but it can be a really good aid in a different way. A critical voice really picks up momentum during some troubled time in our lives, often our early lives.

Experts in child development say that a critical voice often begins around the age of four or five. By then, we have a fairly sophisticated level of language and enough understanding of the world to begin to want to have strategies to negotiate it.

Four-year-olds are inclined to pretty black and white thinking. If you notice that your critical voice tends to see things in fairly all or nothing terms, that could be why. Sometimes a critical voice is a way a child might begin to punish himself or herself as a kind of pre-emptive strike. If they get in first and give themselves a bad time, it might save them from being punished by a parent or carer. When this is true, tapping on the negative emotional charge that still clings to traumatic experiences around that time will help to take away their intensity. After all, who wants their decisions to be being made or even influenced by a four-year-old? What if it is your four-year-old self deciding what you can do and where you should and should not go?

Exactly what the words are that you choose to criticize yourself with may give you some clues. Ask yourself how you feel when you hear certain words and phrases from that critical voice. Close your eyes and really focus on those feelings. Let your mind drift back to when you had a feeling like that before. It may just take you back to an experience or a series of experiences that it would be really useful to tap on. (Remember The Movie Technique? If not, give yourself a refresher by having a look at Appendix A at the back of the book.)

Our teens are another time when we are vulnerable to the impact of experiences that we have. It is a time when we are establishing who we are and how the world is. If your critical voice is angry and impatient, this may have been when it was formed. That would be your cue to start looking at what happened in your teens that may have left an emotional legacy you would be better off if you could shed.

Janice was a 45-year-old mother of two. She had stayed home for several years when her children were young, as she wanted to give them the attention and support that she felt her mother had never been available to give her. She really enjoyed her time with her children but it was over-shadowed by her doubts about whether she was getting it right.

Her inner critic would tell her, 'You are not a good mother. You are not as good a mother as Joan. She has much more patience. Or you are not as good a mother as Becky. Her children can count and read.' At the school gate it was even worse. Her inner critic would tell her that other mothers were better dressed than she was, that the other mothers would not want her in their group.

But her inner turmoil really went into overdrive when she wanted to go back to work. Job applications, doing her CV, interviews – they pushed her inner critic into a frenzy. She felt she had to do something to change it.

Janice started by doing her Personal Peace Plan (you can find a more detailed outline of this in the previous chapter). As she did, the critical voice began to lose its strident hold on her. Then she did a lot of tapping like the tap-along above. She wanted to get her Inner Critic on her side. Finally she took some of the phrases that came up often

– 'they will never choose you', for example, and said them over and over, noticing where and how they made her feel in her body. Then she focussed on that feeling and let her mind drift back to the earliest memory it reminded her of. It was of being left until last when children were picking who to have on their skipping teams. She neutralized that with the Movie Technique.

She still has a critical voice. But it is more gently spoken. It is more moderate in its warnings. And now when she hears it, Janice stops to take stock of whether it has a helpful message for her, rather than fighting it or cringing from it, or letting it run her life. Sometimes it does have a legitimate warning for her. Sometimes it is just like a cracked old record and she thanks it and moves on. And she is really enjoying her new career.

 When you turn down the volume of your critical voice and soften its vocabulary, you will be amazed how much more confident you will feel. It will be much easier to believe you can do things you have never tried before, and to mix with people in a more comfortable way.

8. Tapping with children

When things are bothering children they make great tappers because they can try new things with an open mind, even if those new things seem somewhat bizarre to adults. And usually they are uninhibited about sharing it with their friends.

It is never too early to start. You can use EFT on a newborn baby, with just slight modification. It is better to go for a gentle pressure on each point, rather than tapping, and you should skip the crown of the head point because that part of a newborn baby's skull is so vulnerable. Don't worry that a baby does not yet have language to express its emotions with. The point of words in EFT is to keep our attention on what it is that we want to tap on. As adults, we tend to have multi-track minds. But a distressed baby has total focus on whatever he or she is crying about, so their attention will stay there without any need for external prompting.

 Hilary was having EFT therapy for herself and happened to mention how little sleep she was getting because her baby was such a difficult sleeper. This had come as a shock, as her first child had been placid, and slept through the night almost from the day he was born.

But her new baby seemed unable to go to sleep or to stay asleep. He would cry for hours at bedtime. When he finally went to sleep, it would be to wake and cry a short time later. She and her husband were exhausted and at their wits' end.

Her therapist suggested that she try some gentle EFT at bedtime – just pressing and holding each point in turn. The result seemed little short of a miracle. After a couple of nights, her baby slept for eight hours for the first time in his life. Whatever was causing the sleep problems, EFT resolved it.

TAPPING WITH CHILDREN STRATEGIES

- Beyond infancy, the trick is to adapt EFT to the age and stage of the child. A toddler with no idea what numbers mean could indicate how bad something feels with their hands – wide apart for a ten, closed for a zero and whatever it is in between.

- Usually, as soon as they have got the idea of what numbers stand for, children really love using them.

- Language needs to be adapted, too. A young child does not understand, 'I deeply and completely accept myself'. To know what they will, listen to their language. They will get something like 'I'm a great kid.'

- Tapping can be really helpful in or in preparation for any situation a child finds stressful, or even frightening. They may be happy to be tapped on, or they may like to learn to do it for themselves. Being tapped on may transition into tapping on themselves as they get older.

- Teenagers often love it. They are at a time in their lives when they have little control over their lives or even themselves. Hormones rage, and sweep reason out of the picture. They think they're adults, but also feel like children. Learning EFT can give them a tool that enables them to have control of one thing in their lives – themselves.

 Some parents like to do a Peace Plan for their children at bedtime. When you have put your son or daughter to bed at night, take a little time – maybe before or after a bedtime story – to sit with them and ask them to tell you all about their day. This is not about what was good or bad. Just 'tell me what happened to you today'.

As the child tells, you tap. Exactly how depends on what your child seems to be happy with. So it might be just holding their hand and tapping the side of the hand point while they talk. Or it might be just tapping on one particular point, if they like that more than others. A bit of trial and error will establish what your child enjoys.

What it means is that they draw their own attention to the good things about the day and they are able to detach their negative emotions from the bad. What counts as 'bad' is not always obvious to someone looking in from the outside. A child may be talking about how someone else was told off for something that they themselves got away with but, below the surface, they may be feeling anxious as they talk about it, that another time it could happen to them. Whatever comes up, they will be clearing the disruption to their thoughts before they sleep.

Tony was a fifteen-year-old with a bad name. He had had a teacher who did not like him. The feeling was mutual. They clashed in class, and the teacher made sure that his reputation went ahead of him into all his new classes.

Tony was smart enough to know that the report he got when he left school could be make or break when he applied for the apprenticeship he wanted. He was also smart enough to know that he could not change the way his teachers were treating him. He could only change the way he responded. But how?

One teacher in particular blamed him for everything that happened in class, even if it had been absolutely nothing to do with him. He would flare up and take himself and his anger out of the classroom. He was in danger of being suspended, or even excluded.

A school counsellor taught him to use EFT. He loved the way it let him choose how to respond, and he loved the feeling that he was 'getting one over' on the teacher, who could no longer provoke him, and he got his apprenticeship.

---

9. Tapping for two

Tapping in twos can be a powerful way to use EFT. You and your tapping buddy can offer one another support, as well as the benefit of an objective view as you work through what is troubling you. Often someone else can see what we cannot see ourselves, because we are just too close to a problem.

Team up with a friend and you can take it in turns to be the one taking the lead and the one following. For simplicity and clarity, I'm going to call one partner the 'therapist' and the other partner the 'client'. There are two different ways you can do this. You and your buddy can tap either with or on each other.

Tapping with another person:
1. Sit a comfortable distance apart. Take some time to tune in to one another. Matching your posture to each other's and letting your breathing settle into a similar pattern will build a sense of rapport between you.

2. Together, work out a set-up statement. One of the advantages of a buddy is that we will often spontaneously use striking or resonant phrases that really get to the heart of the matter. But if we try to formulate the 'right' set-up we may find that the words no longer flow as they did. When coming up with words, we may not

even realize what we said, and a therapist buddy can help by reminding us of some of the ways we described what we are feeling and helping us weave them into a useful set-up statement.

3. If you are the therapist and your partner describes an emotion, remind them to link it with the location and sensation – where and how they feel it in their body – and work out together how to incorporate that into the set-up.

4. Rate on a scale of 1–10 how bad this feels. The therapist buddy can make a note of it.

5. The therapist now takes the lead in tapping. So he or she will say the set-up statement three times and tap on it, and the client repeats the words and taps on them, too.

So let's say the set-up you agreed was, 'Even though I have this dull red ball of rage in the pit of my stomach, I deeply and completely accept myself.'

The therapist would tap on their own side of the hand point, on the side of the hand, while saying 'Even though I have this dull red ball of rage in the pit of my stomach ...'. The client would then tap on the same point and repeat the same words. The therapist would then say, 'I deeply and completely accept myself'. The client then taps and repeats.

The therapist would then use the reminder phrase, in this case, 'This dull red ball of rage in the pit of my stomach' and tap around the points from the top of the head to the underarm, twice, saying the reminder phrase on each one and pausing on each one to let the client repeat it on each point.

 When you're tapping with someone else, you want to go at the speed that is comfortable for them. Some people tap really quickly and others like it to be slower. You can ask, or better, guess how fast or slow this 'client' is likely to be. You can get clues from the speed at which they move and speak in other contexts. Then you can just watch carefully and see if the person you are tapping with is getting ahead of you or behind you. If they are, slow down or speed up accordingly.

Tapping on another person

1. The procedure is much the same here. If you agree to tap on another person, you may need to sit closer to be able to reach comfortably to tap on your partner. Then you build rapport, rate on a scale of 1–10, and work out the set-up statement and reminder phrase in just the same way.

2. Now, the therapist taking the lead taps on the client and says the words first and the client buddy repeats them.

3. If you are tapping, do it quite firmly but not so hard that it is uncomfortable, let alone painful, for your client. Check with your buddy if the pressure is okay with them.

 When you are the one saying the words first, you say them as if you are your partner. You both know the words refer to the other person, but you say them as if you are them so they do not have to re-word what you say. They just repeat it.

You will not 'catch' your buddy's problem by tapping on it as if it's yours. Quite the reverse. You may find that as you tap with and for them, things that are troubling you but that you have put to the back of your mind are cleared at the same time.

---

10. Have a nice day

EFT is a great way to deal with problems, to improve health, to manage anxiety and to enhance performance. All of this sounds complicated, but it essentially leads to one thing: the ability to simply have a nice day. What we're going to do now is go through a typical 'day in the life' and see how tapping might help in everyday situations.

1. Tapping on restricted breathing

When you get up, stand by your bed or in the bathroom or the kitchen and take a really deep breath. Take the deepest breath that you can. As you do, notice if it feels as if it is a really full breath or if, at some point, it seems to hit an obstruction.

If it's not a ten out of ten breath – and few people find that it is – rate it. Was it seven out of ten? Or eight? Or three? At the point where it felt it could go no further how did it feel as if it was being restricted? Did it feel as if your ribs would not open wide enough? Or as if the breath hit a wall? Or as if you were holding on in some way? Whatever you experience, describe it and tap on it. So it might be, 'Even though it feels as if my breath hits a brick wall, I deeply and completely accept myself,' with the reminder phrase, 'My breath hits a brick wall'.

If, after the first round, it is still not a ten out of ten breath, do you need to change the description? Does it still feel as if you hit a brick wall, or as if your breath had to swim uphill, for example?

Sometimes when you do this it will just liven up your energy system and maybe get rid of underlying issues harming it, without your even being aware of what it is that you have cleared. Other times it might spontaneously bring into your awareness something you need to deal with more specifically. Either way it can help set you up for the day.

2. Tapping on the challenge of the day

What is going to be the most challenging thing on today's programme? Tap on how you feel about the prospect of it. A good place to do this is in the shower. So maybe something along the lines of: 'Even though I have this heavy dread in my stomach when I think about that meeting this afternoon ...', or 'Even though I'm going to have to talk to my son's teacher and I am really anxious in my chest about it ...', or any of the hundred variations we might be going to have to deal with through the day.

3. Tapping to keep stress at bay

Take a minute from time to time through the day to take stock. Sit quietly. Close your eyes. Just for a minute or two let yourself notice whatever grabs your attention. Is it a thought? A feeling? Tension in your shoulders? A fluttery tightness in your gut? Just notice, without judging it, and then tap on it. So it might be: 'Even though my shoulders feel hunched up, as if I am about to go into battle, I accept myself without judgment.'

Without judgment is a good phrase in this context. You do not necessarily want to be distracted for long from what you were doing at this point in the day. You just want to notice and stop stress building your tension up.

4. Tap as you need

If anything upsets or challenges you through the day, tap if you can. If you cannot do it openly, imagine you are doing it. Or do something surreptitiously, like tapping on the side of the hand point under the desk.

5. Be grateful

Take ten minutes – near bedtime is a good time to do this – to do your gratitude list. Write down the things you're grateful for. When you do, you raise your levels of positive energy and pave the way for more good things to come to you.

6. Sleep well

Insomnia can greatly damage your quality of life. Sleeping well is so important that it has a whole chapter of its own in this book (chapter 23), but if you are worried that you will have trouble sleeping tonight stop right here and tap on that fear.

So your phrase might be: 'Even though I feel really anxious in the pit of my stomach when I think about getting to sleep tonight ...'. Or it might be: 'Even though I feel so angry in my shoulders that I am having so many bad nights' sleep ...'. Or it might be: 'Even though I'm so afraid that I will lie there hour after hour ...'.

PART TWO
EFT for anxiety

---

11. What is anxiety?

Do some situations make you anxious? Do you feel a sense of panic when you're in crowded places? Does the idea of making a presentation really freak you out? Do you feel uneasy around other people? Or perhaps you have a phobia of something like spiders or birds or frogs? Have you had or do you have full-on panic attacks? Or is your holiday overshadowed or your promotion prospects handicapped by the dread of making a flight? EFT can be a huge help in beating anxiety in all its guises.

In this part of the book you will discover how EFT can help with:

- panic attacks
- travel anxiety
- fear of flying
- phobias
- sports performance
- presentations
- examinations

 When you want to get rid of anxiety *symptoms* you are feeling, tapping on 'Even though I have this anxiety ...', or 'Even though I feel anxious ...' is not the best way to do it. Instead, try something like,

'Even though I have this big black lump of anxiety in the pit of my stomach …'. We do not actually feel 'anxiety'. We feel something in our bodies that our brains tell us is anxiety. What we need to tap on is what we actually experience.

EFT offers the opportunity to work with anxiety in two different ways. The first is to deal with where it is coming from. That might be a specific frightening event that has left you hyper-vigilant and on hair-trigger alert for danger. Or it might be a series of experiences when you were young that interfered with your ability to learn to trust yourself to be safe in the world, or left you believing the world is never a safe place. If it's a simple phobia, it might have been a single traumatic incident – though we may have learned it by being around someone, often our mother, who had the same fear. So EFT can be useful alongside detective work to find the underlying causes of our anxiety and deal with them.

The second way EFT helps is by giving us control over our anxiety symptoms when and where we feel them.

We have the problem of living with what are really primitive bodies in the high stress 21st century. We come pre-programmed to undergo changes to our bodies, which we experience as anxiety symptoms, when we encounter what we *feel* is a threat. We don't even have to be consciously aware that that is what we feel. It may contradict what we *think*. The threat response system automatically kicks in and does what it sees as its job – to protect us from what it sees as danger. The response is the same whether it is physical or psychological danger.

Before looking in more detail at how to work with EFT to banish or reduce anxiety, you may find it useful to follow me on a brief detour into how the nervous system operates. We used to think that we had only one threat defence system – the fight or flight response. We thought that when something seemed threatening, the sympathetic nervous system turned it on. And when we felt the danger was over the parasympathetic half of the nervous system switched it off and got us back on an even keel again. It is still true that this system explains most of our 'everyday' anxiety responses. It is about 300,000 years old. To put that into perspective, *Homo sapiens* has only been around for about 200,000 years.

But the bigger picture has changed, thanks to the work of a remarkable man called Stephen Porges, director of the Brain Body Center at the University of Illinois, whose speciality is biological psychology, and what he has called the Polyvagal theory. This theory says the parasympathetic nervous system plays a game of two halves. Most experts now accept his theory that the parasympathetic nervous system is run by the two-part vagus nerve. The back half of it, which links gut and brain, goes back about 500,000 years and began in fish before it moved on to reptiles and is still around in us. Its response to extreme stress is to slow down, and possibly even shut down. Its mode is conservation. It has to take the rap for people who faint when they are frightened enough, or who find themselves unable to move, frozen to the spot when they feel fear. The front half of the vagus nerve is the relative newcomer, only around for the last 80,000 years, and links middle ear, throat and face. It is the social engagement system, and it is unique to mammals.

So how does this work in practice? Say, for example, you think someone is trying to lull you into letting your guard down because they are getting ready to snatch your phone. Instinctively, you might first try to smile at them and to engage them as a human being, to win them over so they leave you alone. That is the front part of the vagus system at work.

When that is failing, or when you unconsciously consider it for a split second and dismiss that as a possibility, the sympathetic nervous system might switch you into fight or flight mode, with adrenaline giving you an energy boost and increasing blood flow to your legs so you can run or your fists so you can fight, or both. At the same time blood flow to the brain decreases so we cannot think clearly and logically. And, finally as you realize that he is bigger and meaner than you and has a knife, and you have no hope of escape, you might find yourself unable to do anything. Your system might go into a hopeless phase. You might even faint.

Fight or flight still rules. Fight or flight is where most of our day-to-day experience of anxiety comes from. It is, as it says on the tin, designed to help us put maximum physical effort into fighting off or getting away from an attacking animal or member of the neighbouring rival tribe. It takes all the blood flow to the muscles we need to use to defend ourselves or get away from the danger. It shuts down the higher levels of the brain, making us temporarily stupid.

So despite our deepening understanding of our internal defences, fight or flight is still where much of the action is. And its ability to shut down our higher reasoning was a good design feature because no-one trying to out-run a tiger needs to be doing calculus at the same time. But that means that when we feel fear we cannot reason our way out of a situation, as we normally would.

These days, when the fight or flight response is triggered to some degree, we are often not in physical danger. We might be stressed by a difficult boss and afraid we will be the one made redundant if we do not meet his unreasonable demands, for example.

When the fight or flight system is switched on, it is not only the nervous system that is affected. It is potentially a whole body experience. Hormones including adrenaline and cortisol are released. They speed up heart rate and breathing, constrict blood vessels and tighten muscles, which gives the body a burst of extra strength.

At the extreme, these reactions account for those otherwise inexplicable bursts of strength that have enabled someone to lift a weight way beyond their normal maximum capability to save the life of a child, for example, or a wounded soldier to carry a more badly-injured comrade a long way to medical help. On the negative side, immune function shuts down, too, which is why someone who is highly stressed over a long period of time is more prone to catching everything that is going around and less quick to recover.

Have a look at the list below and see how many you have experienced. You may recognize here some of the symptoms of panic attacks and the seeds of IBS (irritable bowel syndrome).

- Slow digestion
- Dry mouth
- Shortness of breath
- Being pale or flushed
- Feeling hot and cold
- Need to urinate
- Reduced hearing
- Reduced peripheral vision
- Shakiness
- Loss of bowel control
- Nausea or abdominal distress
- Numbness or tingling in hands and feet
- Feeling not quite real/outside the body
- Dizziness and faintness
- Erectile dysfunction

- Racing heart
- Chest pain
- Reduced immune system
- High blood pressure
- Sweating

Natural selection will have ensured that the people who were most on hair-trigger alert for danger and most physically responsive when they detected it were most likely to survive to contribute to the gene pool. In other words, our most anxious ancestors had an advantage over the more laid back, so we are more likely to have got our genes from the more fearful ones.

The trouble is that we are now, mostly, not in danger from wild animals or warlike neighbouring tribes. The response our bodies make is no longer appropriate for the action we need to take. If we do not understand what is going on it adds another layer of concern to crank up our anxiety – anxiety about anxiety.

 There are lifestyle choices that contribute to anxiety, and which it makes sense to look at first.

If you feel anxious the morning after a heavy night before, you might consider changing your drinking habits. Tapping will help with the hangover, but the next time you drink too much you have a hangover again. The same can be true for recreational drugs. In some people they cause panic attacks. Or, you may wake in panic the next morning. Equally, if you are drinking too much coffee anxiety may disappear or decrease if you cut back.

Trying to deal with anxiety while continuing to do what you know makes you anxious is a bit like swimming upstream with your hands tied behind your back.

Fight or flight is designed to help us put maximum physical effort into fighting off or getting away from an attacking animal or member of the neighbouring rival tribe. But those body changes really do not help in most modern contexts. This lies behind the many experiences of anxiety described in the following chapters.

12. Panic attacks

Panic attacks are really frightening. If you have one for the first time the fear about what is happening to you will amplify the volume of the symptoms. If you have never had one before and also don't know what a panic attack is it may be an even more terrifying experience.

Typically, sufferers say that they thought they were either having a heart attack or going mad or both. They are not. A surprisingly large number of people have them at some time in their lives. Ask in any Accident and Emergency department and they will tell you that many people go there when they are experiencing panic because they are convinced they are in the middle of a medical emergency.

Even when it has happened before, and they have been to casualty before, they may still be unable to believe it's 'only' a panic attack, and people who have had panic attacks are often are so afraid that they will have another that that expectation triggers one. It becomes a self-perpetuating vicious circle. The EFT action plan includes any or all of the following. You choose what seems relevant for you.

PANIC ATTACK STRATEGIES

In the moment:

• Make a fist and **lightly thump the point in the centre of the chest** where a man would knot his tie. Or, if you prefer, tap the side of the hand point.

If you are having a panic attack, it's highly unlikely that you will be able to think clearly enough to do any full-on tapping with a set-up statement and reminder phrase. So until you can bring you panic level down low enough to think, the centre of the chest point is a useful quick anxiety stopper.

OR

- Just tap on the side of the hand point. Again, don't worry about the words.

OR

- Tap around the points without worrying about the words and without worrying whether you miss any. When you're as tuned in to your feelings as you will be if you are having a panic attack, you do not need words to keep your attention on your feelings. You will be tuned in already.

In the aftermath:

- **After the worst** of the panic has subsided, you need to start serious tapping on the feelings left in your body. So take stock. What do you feel where? Tension? Shakiness? Fear? Where do you feel it? How do you feel it?

So you might now be tapping on something like: 'Even though I have this shaky feeling in my arms and legs I deeply and completely accept myself,' or 'Even though I still have this scared feeling in the middle of my gut, I deeply and completely accept myself.'

- Ask yourself if the feelings remind you of anything. Have you had this feeling years ago, in a different context? If you can pinpoint what and when, that should also be a tapping target. If you don't immediately get anything, then try closing your eyes and just focussing on the feeling and letting your mind gently drift back. No pressure. It does not matter if you do not get anything

EFT has this brilliant habit of showing us where we need to go. While you are tapping on the left-over sensations from a panic attack, it is particularly important to take note of anything, particularly any memory that comes into your mind. If this happens, it is not your mind wandering. It is your unconscious mind telling you: 'This is linked. Deal with it.' Similarly if you can identify when you have had the feeling in the past, it pinpoints another useful tapping target.

- When you feel calmer, **try to remember** what you felt just before it became full-on panic. This is really important information to have.

Once you recognize the early warning signs, you are in a really strong position to take charge. In future, as soon as you feel any hint of a possible approaching wave of anxiety, whether it is a thought or a feeling, tap on it. Zap it before it can go any further. It might be, for example, 'Even though I have this sudden sinking darkness in the pit of my stomach, I deeply and completely accept myself.' Or if you feel something that you recognize as the start of a previous panic attack just focus on it and tap and don't bother about the words.

Then throw in a few rounds of the following: 'Even though I have this feeling, I know what this is. It is only anxiety and anxiety cannot hurt me. And I accept myself anyway.' Repeat that three times while you tap on the side of the hand point. Then go round the points alternating the reminder phrases, 'this is only anxiety' and 'anxiety cannot hurt me'.

To immunize yourself:

- Treat **past panic attacks** as if they were individual traumatic events, and process them with EFT in the way described in chapter 5 or the reminder in Appendix A. Make sure you keep going until you can tell these stories without any remaining emotion.

The specific panic attacks that it's usually most useful to process in this way are:

- The first or first you remember
- The worst
- The most recent or most recent really bad one

Subsequently, whenever you have one, when you are calm enough again, treat it the same way.

Because our response to cues from the environment – and that means both the world around us and our own internal environment – is determined by our past experiences, it's really helpful to have taken as much as we can of the negative emotion from those past experiences that our brain automatically uses for reference to determine whether we are safe or in danger.

- **Clear all your old traumas** in the same way. Pay particular attention, in this context, to traumas in which you were really in physical danger. Have you been in a car accident? Have you been attacked?

- Then do your Personal Peace Plan, as described in chapter 6. That will not only help get rid of the root of your anxiety but will probably clear most other possible difficulties you have as well.

 Alan was a 33-year-old plasterer who came to see me because he was constantly anxious and had had several panic attacks. He lived in dread that he would have more. He had been on a fairly even keel most of his adult life. He liked a few pints on a Friday night with his mates, but he had never used recreational drugs.

Then one night he went to a club and friends persuaded

him to try ecstasy for the first time. Next morning he woke up having a massive panic attack, which was also a first for him. It left him feeling terrified that it would happen again. The fear of having another panic attack actually caused a few more, though not of quite the same high intensity.

The first thing we did together was to do the Movie Technique, to disempower the memory of the first attack. Then we processed the others.

He learned that when he felt even the slightest trace of anxiety symptoms he should stop what he was doing and tap until he got rid of it. Sometimes at work he would hide in the lavatory to do this. He would also tap on, 'Even though I have this feeling (which he described) I know it is only anxiety and anxiety cannot hurt me and I accept myself anyway.'

After a few weeks, Alan was able to put panic attacks and anxiety at a level that seemed quite abnormal to him behind him.

13. Travel anxiety

Complex travel anxiety

Complex travel anxiety is a term I use for a type of anxiety I have often come across in my practice. I suspect that people who live in large cities are particularly vulnerable to it and this may explain why I see so many people with this in my practice in London. It refers to people who have a whole string of things they can no longer do, or can do only by gritting their teeth and suffering.

Typically, it includes travelling on trains, on the underground, or overground. People who have it feel they cannot catch a bus or drive over high bridges or through tunnels or even in any car they are not driving themselves. Often they cannot get in a lift. Complex travel anxiety most often starts with one of these and then spreads.

So perhaps it began with someone going down the escalator to a London underground platform in the rush hour on a hot day. It was crowded. They felt uncomfortable physical sensations. They were hot. They felt they could not really breathe. They felt as if they were having a panic attack …

They didn't realize they felt that way just because it was unpleasantly hot and crowded. So the expectation of a repeat panic attack made them unable to get into a crowded carriage. And then they became unable to go into an uncrowded carriage. And then it became impossible to go down the escalator at all.

Unchallenged, the next thing will be that they cannot go on any train. And so on. The end point would be agoraphobia – refusing to leave the house at all. That is unless they fight back.

COMPLEX TRAVEL ANXIETY STRATEGIES

- **Make a list** of everything you feel unable to do. Put them into a hierarchy of difficulty. What on the list would be the least difficult to do? Then rank them in order up to the most difficult. Include even small stuff. If you cannot catch a train, can you go to the station and not get on a train? Could you go and stand on a platform? Could you go to the station and get on a train and go just one stop, if it wasn't rush hour? What about if you had someone you trust with you?

Once you have your list pick the least difficult to start with. Imagine yourself doing it. What feelings come up just imagining it? Tap until they subside. Persist if you need to. If you really cannot get them low or zero just thinking about it, can you break it down to an even smaller step? Then do it.

Remember now that when you take the first step, you no longer have to just tough it out. You have EFT to help you. And remember if you are somewhere you feel you cannot tap, you can just tap the side of the hand point. Or you can tap the gamut point, on the back of the hand when you make a fist just below the little finger and ring finger joints. Or you can thump where a man would knot his tie. You can even imagine tapping. By now your unconscious mind will know what it is that you are imagining.

Work through each step on your list of what you cannot do, one at a time. Tap on the feelings that come up in advance, and tap as you do it. If you feel this attempt goes really badly then tap on the memory of it going really badly and then start again. As each one is cleared, move to the next.

- **What else was happening at the time** your problem started? That will often give you good clues to other issues you need to tap on.

- **Work through all the panic attack strategies.** Most of them will be relevant for you, too. Pay particular attention to any travel-related traumas in your history. Remember to include traumas that did not happen to you. Did you watch on television or read about a travel accident and imagine it so vividly that it's almost as if it happened to you? Process the memory as if it was really yours.

Janet was a 40-year-old PA in Canary Wharf in London who was no longer able to travel on the underground. Her problem started apparently

79

out of the blue. She couldn't remember anything about it starting; it was simply not there one day and there the next. When we looked at what else was happening at the time, she said she had first felt it in the school summer holidays in 2005 and it had been gradually getting worse ever since.

On 7 July that year, four bombs went off on the London underground and one on a double-decker bus. There were 52 people killed and more than 700 injured. I asked her how vividly she remembered it. Janet had watched the television footage and read the newspapers, and she had stored such vivid 'memories' in her head that it was almost as if she had been there. Ever since, her unconscious mind had been doing its best to keep her safe by making sure she did not suffer the same fate. It 'knew' she would be safer if she did not go on underground trains. She was caught between consciously understanding that it was safe and unconsciously being terrified of that 'remembered' trauma.

Once we dealt with those memories as if they really were hers, she was able to begin working through her hierarchy of things she had been unable to do and one by one, with guts and tenacity, she found she could do them again.

Fear of flying

Flying is much safer than driving. We are more likely to have an accident driving to the airport than we are to have one in the air. Most people who have a fear of flying know that, but it makes little or no difference. Logically they know they are no less safe than they are crossing the street. But at another level, the prospect terrifies them.

They also know that turbulence is just bumpy air, no more dangerous in a modern aircraft built to withstand much worse, than going over a bump in the road. It is not life-threatening. The worst that can happen is a minor injury to anyone who ignores the seat belt sign.

Not everyone who is afraid of flying is suffering in the same way. Everyone is different. Their beliefs are different. The sensations are different. They can vary from needing a stiff drink or a prescription for Valium to get them into the aircraft to feeling they would kill someone to get out. And many people would not even book a flight in the first place.

For some it is a fear of crashing and dying. For others it is a fear of crashing and not dying. It can be a fear of dying and leaving their family without their care. It can be a fear that they will fall out of the floor or the plane will fall out of the sky.

They may be most afraid of take-off or landing or hitting turbulence.

Perhaps the most frequent fears I meet when I work with people who are afraid to fly are fears of losing control of themselves and having a panic attack, and the fear of being confined in an aircraft with absolutely no control over the duration. On a train, you can get off at the next station. On an aircraft, the doors are closed. The windows don't open. No matter how much you want to, you cannot get out until the pilot decides you can.

FEAR OF FLYING STRATEGIES

- **Make a list of everything** you can think of that is involved in your fear. Is it being confined? Is it being afraid of take-off? Is it the sound of the engine? Is it changes in engine sound? These need to be your tapping targets, one at a time. Imagine each, notice the feelings that come up, and tap and tap until they disappear.

- **Have you had a bad flight?** Were you untroubled about flying until that return flight from Spain when it was really bumpy? Or that time the pilot said you had to burn up fuel before landing because there could be a problem with the landing gear? If so, start by dealing with the worst moments of that past experience with the Movie Technique described in detail in chapters 5 and 24, or in Appendix A.

- **Notice when it starts.** If you know you're really anxious on flights, notice when the very first twinge starts. Is it when you book? If so, tap before, during and after booking. Is it when you start to pack? When you get to the check-in? Don't let it build up. Tap as soon as you notice so you can keep on top of it.

- **Go back to the panic attack strategies discussed in the previous chapter and work through them.** Once you know how to tap with anxiety in the moment, you are on the way to being back in control of yourself.

14. Phobias

As mentioned earlier, it was a phobia that really deserves the credit for the invention of EFT. Roger Callahan, founder of TFT from which EFT evolved, first starting tapping on clients after he found it cleared the previously intractable water phobia of a client called Mary.

A phobia is an irrational or exaggerated fear of some object or situation. A phobia sufferer's response to whatever they are phobic about can range from mild but unpleasant discomfort all the way up to terror so instant and uncontrollable that they would run into the road without pausing to check for traffic to get away from the source of the overwhelming fear.

People who have a phobia often believe, in their rational thinking minds, that whatever it is they are phobic about is harmless. Ask them on a scale of 1–10 how dangerous they believe it to be and they will say zero. But ask them how harmless it *feels* and you will get a completely different answer. It could be as high as a ten.

Arachnophobia, or fear of spiders, is one of the most widespread phobias, even in countries where the spiders are not dangerous at all. But there are hundreds and hundreds of phobias. People are really terrified of snakes and crabs and the dark and vomiting and noise and needles and insects and buttons … The list could go on and on.

When someone has a fear of spiders they may unable to go into a room at all if they believe there is a spider in it. A person with a snake phobia might run into the traffic without looking either way if they see a snake charmer on the pavement way up the road, or a frog phobia may make them unable to bear seeing even a picture of a frog, let alone a real, live one.

The traditional view of a phobia is that it is one-shot learning. Something happens, we have an immediate and extreme reaction to it, and we never forget it. From that moment on we go on having the same reaction to the same thing. That can be true. But we now realize that it's not always as simple as that. Some people have the same phobia as a mother or father did. Coincidence? Hereditary? Much more likely they learned to be afraid of something by sensing their parent's fear every time that thing was around.

Even when it's the one-shot learning it can be mistaken learning. Sometimes a person becomes phobic about something that they were watching or eating or hearing or seeing when something really upsetting, but quite unrelated to it, happened. The focus of their attention at that moment may be quite unrelated to whatever caused the fear but somehow the fear gets hooked to it and it gets to be the subject of their phobia. If you are trying to work out where your phobia started, you need to bear that possibility in mind.

CASE STUDY

When Patricia was seven, she was in her bedroom one night watching her pet hamster in its cage. Suddenly, her father burst into the room. He had been drinking all evening, as he often did, and he hit her for no reason at all. She was already on edge; she always was when he was drinking because she never knew how he would be.

Somehow she transferred the anger and shock that she felt to the hamster that she had been paying attention to, perhaps because it would have been too dangerous to feel the anger and fear against her father. It left her with an irrational and disproportionate fear of hamsters. But it was not until many years later, when she was tapping on her phobia, that she was able to make that connection and overcome her long-standing fear.

PHOBIA STRATEGIES

- Make a list of everything you can think of that bothers you about whatever it is you're afraid of. Tap on them systematically, one after another, until the one you have been working on no longer bothers you. As you clear each aspect, you may discover others just pop up. You may not be aware of them all at the start.

- If you remember the first time you had this phobic response, treat it as if it were a traumatic memory and do the Movie Technique on it.

- Do the same with the worst episode you can remember. And the worst recent one.

- Finding a picture of what freaks you out on the internet can give you a useful tapping target.

- Imagine your next meeting with the thing that you're phobic about. See if negative feelings still come up. If they do, you are not yet done tapping.

- When your fear is of a situation rather than an object – say fear of heights or fear of the dark – then you need to tap on all the different thoughts and feelings that come up about it.

  Going into the situation can be really productive here. But you can be kind to yourself and do it in stages.

  So, for example, if you're afraid of heights you could go to the height that really triggers you in stages and tap on the unease you feel as soon as you feel it and before it ramps up to full-on fear.

- It is also useful with variations like fear of heights or fear of enclosed spaces to really notice the feeling it gives you, focus on it and let your mind drift back as far as you can to when you know that you had a feeling like that before.

  If you identify a time, tap on it. Then see if it is possible to drift back even further to an even earlier time and do it again.

USEFUL TIP

It is hard to be sure if you have got rid of all the aspects of a phobia until you're back in the situation. Even imagining it is not a fool-proof test. But if you discover, when you are next confronted by the thing you were so afraid of, that you still have more to do, you now have a tool to do it with. Tap at once. The best time is when you have the feelings fresh in your system.

15. Improve your performance

Do you hate making presentations so much that you would avoid a promotion so you did not have to do them? Or call in sick at the last minute so a colleague has to step in? Or feel as if you are carrying a big black cloud around with you when you know you have one coming up? Do you wait your turn to introduce yourself at a workshop with mounting dread? Are exams your bugbear? Do you get so anxious that you can't remember things you know you know? Or is your performance in your sport reduced by how anxious you are about doing the best you can?

One thing it is important to bear in mind is that presenting, doing exams and competing in sport are not the best they can be when we are completely calm and relaxed. We all have an optimal level of arousal and fear in our systems – a level at which we perform best. Actors say that if they don't feel like throwing up before the curtain goes up on an opening night, the show will flop. The trick is to know the level at which you perform best and to use tapping to get you there.

PERFORMANCE ANXIETY STRATEGIES

- Try to remember any time **when you were a child at home or at school**, when you were involved in some kind of 'performance' and it bombed. Were you doing your party piece for visitors and your mother told you to stop showing off? Do you remember reading aloud in class and a classmate sniggered or a teacher snapped at you? Did you go blank in a school play? Or play the wrong notes in a school concert?

If so, treat it as a traumatic memory and do the Movie Technique on it. If you have more than one such memory work through them all. However much you try to tell yourself it was no big deal, if it was to you then, to your unconscious mind, it still is now.

- If you have had **student or adult experiences** of making presentations or speeches or speaking in meetings that you felt really did not go well, treat in the same way.

- Mentally rehearse the situation. Imagine you are up on the stage at the mike (or whatever is relevant) and let the nerves come. Invite them to come on. Then tap to get rid of the excess. Keep doing it until it is hard to access the emotions at all.

- For presentations **rehearse the opening**. How much you'll need to rehearse the rest of your presentation will vary. If you know your subject inside out you may need only a few headlines on PowerPoint or a scrap of paper to keep you focussed on the plot. Or if you are less experienced or less familiar with the material you are presenting you may need to rehearse more. Whichever end of the spectrum you are, get your opening few sentences off by heart and rehearsed until you can say them in your sleep. And practice taking a slow **deep breath** before you start.

REMEMBER THIS!!! If you are too anxious when you start speaking, you may have trouble keeping your brain in gear. Remember that when the fight or flight response kicks in it makes us stupid. So right at the start, it is really useful not to have to think. Give your nervous system a bit of a crutch while you calm yourself down by being really over-rehearsed on the opening.

- Start tapping **sooner rather than later**. If you feel nervous at the prospect of an upcoming presentation, tap as soon as you feel the first twinges. It is so much easier to stop the anxiety building up than to banish it once it has.

- **Find** one or two of those people in the audience who always nod or smile in agreement. They will encourage you. And smile back. It'll help you shift your nervous system away from the anxious fight or flight response to the less scary social engagement system described on page 66.

- Don't aspire to be completely calm and relaxed. Remember everyone needs to be a bit hyped up to perform at their best. There is nothing like a bit of extra adrenaline to keep you thinking fast on your feet.

EXAM ANXIETY STRATEGIES

Exam anxiety has a lot of common ground with presentation anxiety, so a lot of the same strategies are relevant. It is another place where being completely relaxed is counter-productive. You need a level of arousal and only you know the right level for you.

Can you recognize a time when you were doing an exam and you really felt as if you were flying? Thoughts came fast. Things you thought you had forgotten seemed to jump out of your memory. Connections made themselves? That is the right level to go for as your tapping target. The better you have prepared for your exam, the more potential anxiety you will have pre-empted. So the first step is good revision techniques.

- **Memory is state-dependent.** When you're learning things you really need to remember imagine first that you are in the exam room. Conversely when you are trying to remember something, imagine you are in the room in which you revised. But even more important than the location in which you learned is the state in which you did so.

  So when you are stressed and struggling, try just **tapping the side of the hand point** as a way to bring yourself into a better focussed and less overwhelmed state.

CASE STUDY This was my own experience of doing exams when I was studying for my psychology degree. When I went into an exam I was always spaced out by the adrenaline flowing through my system. I would get on a train going in the wrong direction. I would have trouble finding my exam number in a large room. But I would then do well in the exam.

One year I decided I did not want to go through all that again, so I invested some time in learning relaxation techniques. I arrived to do the exam much more laid back. And it was the only exam I have ever done that I did not finish! I had learned the hard way that the stress level at which I perform best in those conditions is quite high.

- **Check out your thoughts**. Are you saying things like, 'I always fail', or 'I am no good at exams'? If you are, decide to challenge them.

- **Try to work out where they came from**. Are there specific events you recall that gave you that belief? A teacher who said you would never amount to anything? A parent who criticized your results? If so, tap on it.

EFT can really be your ally when you want your performance to be the best it can be. It can be good first aid in the moment, but the more you have used it in advance in the ways outlined in this chapter, the less you may find you need it on the day.

16. EFT for sport: Upping your game

EFT has been one of the best-kept secrets in sport. Anything that gives a player or a team a slight edge over the opposition is likely to be adopted – and kept under wraps. Why hand an advantage to your opposition? But the word is gradually getting out.

The commentary team at the 2013 US Open in Augusta, one of the biggest and most prestigious events of the golf year, predicted that EFT was about to be big in the game. Their discussion followed seeing Australian golfer Jason Day using EFT before playing a round of the competition in which he came third. Sharp-eyed television viewers have also spotted pre-contest tapping by a wide range of top sportsmen and women including a Formula One racing driver and an international rugby team in the Six Nations contest, the biggest event of the European rugby union year.

It is hardly surprising. Players and coaches alike know how much difference the mental side of performance makes. That is where you find much of what makes the difference between the best and second best at the highest level. But, unlike many of the aids that top players have available to them, EFT is something we can all use, free, whether we run or swim or play tennis or squash or cricket or football or golf or hockey or any other sport.

Our thoughts, feelings, fears, memories of past disappointments, and worry about how well we have recovered from an old injury – they can all crowd in at key moments to take the edge off our performance. We don't even have to be consciously aware of them. These mental barriers can be subtle. You may have a comfort zone that you have not even recognized but a part of you may be really smart at keeping you in it because it sees it as being 'for your own good'.

When Jane retired from her job as an accountant, she finally had time to play as much golf as she wanted. She had been really looking forward to this. She was a natural athlete and knew that, although she was no longer a youngster, she could be in a different league when she had more time to spend on the course. So she could not understand why her handicap seemed to be stuck at 32. Every time she was having a good enough round to reduce it, something went wrong on the last few holes. She could not break the pattern.

She tapped and tapped – and had a sudden realization. She had a comfort zone she had not recognized. It was where she could continue to play with her regular partners. They were all around the same level. Subconsciously, she feared losing their friendship if she was seen to be much better than them.

Once she knew what was going on below the surface she was able to break the pattern. She reduced her handicap, tapped on her fear that her friends would now not want to play with her – and carried on playing with them.

SPORTS PERFORMANCE STRATEGIES

This is another area of performance, like presentations and examinations, where being somewhat hyped is a plus. Have you ever seen an athlete on the starting blocks in a major competition looking relaxed? Remember that excited and anxious are physiological twins, and we all have a personal best level of arousal. Below it, we underperform. Above it, we underperform. The trick is to know the level at which we function best and aim for it.

EFT can help here in two different ways. Are you anxious about your performance? Or are you anxious about the outcome? Or both? When you are considering strategies, think about both.

- **Think of your best performance ever.** Can you remember just how hyped up you were? This is your goal; not no anxiety, but the right level of anxiety. (Sometimes you might need to tap to bring this level up if you feel a bit too flat.)

- **What specifically is bothering you** about how you perform? Whatever it is, tap on it.

- If what is bothering you seems quite **global**, tap on it anyway, and just see what tapping throws up for you.

Tapping works better the more specific we are but often it will take us from global to specific when we give it the chance. It may be a more specific aspect of our performance or it might take you to a memory.

- Remember, any memory you access will be relevant even if it seems not to be. Work through it with the Movie Technique.

- Don't be fooled if the memory is not sports related. It may not be.

- Do you have a memory of **the first time** this happened? That is a candidate for the Movie Technique.

- Do you have a memory of a performance or event that really went wrong? Tap on it.

- What **negative beliefs** do you have about how good you are or how likely you are to do well. Tap on the belief. Can you work out where they came from? Tap on those memories.

PART THREE:
EFT for health

---

17. Optimum health

If you really want to have the best possible health you can, tapping can help you to achieve it. By alleviating stress and improving our energy, EFT can help boost our immune systems when we are fighting off minor illnesses and may help us find our way back from more serious health challenges. It can also clear negative beliefs that are likely to compromise our health or hamper recovery.

Central to the EFT approach to serious diseases is the idea that unresolved emotions may be *a* (note, '*a*' not '*the*') cause of disease. Finding and clearing such emotions will improve the body's ability to heal itself.

 EFT is a wonderful addition to your medicine chest, but do not throw out your prescriptions without consulting your doctor. Tapping is a fantastic adjunct to conventional medical treatment but it's not necessarily a substitute for it. Make sure when you're ill that you see a doctor and get a diagnosis. You may be putting yourself at risk of you don't.

HEALTH STRATEGIES

- Tap on your symptoms. Tap on them one at a time, starting with the worst. Describe it to yourself in as much detail as you can. Access the intensity (1 –10) and rate it. Then tap on it. For example: 'Even though I have this scratchy, uncomfortable feeling in my eyes like having sand in them …'

- You don't have to wait until you're ill to get started. If you are sneezing and have a slightly sore throat and suspect you may be at risk of having a head cold by tomorrow, tap today.

- If you have pain, tap on it in detail. (You can learn more about how to work with pain in the next chapter.)

- If you are having conventional treatment, EFT may still have a place in working with it. For example, many people find that tapping on the side-effects of chemo-therapy helps to decrease or even eradicate them.

- Ask yourself if there is an emotional issue that you have not resolved and which is contributing to your illness or diminishing your body's ability to recover from it. If there is, use tapping to deal with it. If you do not know if there is, just guess. Remember, guessing is a way of making accessible what we know at an unconscious level.

- What emotions do you have about having this condi-tion? Are you angry? Afraid? Sad? Another emotion? Some combination of emotions? Tap on it or on them all.

- Imagine yourself in excellent health. What tail-enders come up? Remember, tail-enders are the 'yes, buts …' that we have consciously or unconsciously when we picture ourselves having what we want or being as we want. These reservations need to be tapped away.

- Does some part of you think you deserve this illness? If so, why? What do you need to do to change that? Do you need to forgive yourself? Make amends for something? Or do you just need to tap on an old and now redundant belief?

- Is there an unconscious upside to having this illness? If there is some gain, can you get the gain in a different way?

- Ask yourself who you would be if you did not have this illness. Does this bring up things you need to tap on?

- Tap often and long if you need to. Prescribe daily tapping for yourself. And be prepared to be persistent.

REMEMBER THIS!!!

This is not your fault …

Whatever experiences, thoughts, beliefs, emotions you have or have had, if you are ill it is <u>not your fault</u>. You have not set out to be ill. You have not chosen to be ill. Blaming yourself for it is misunderstanding the way your body works, and it drains your resources on top of the illness itself.

If you find yourself feeling that somehow you're guilty, do the following tapalong a few times a day for a few days and see if you can now see it in a different light. Remember if you are doing it and your attention just jumps to a different issue, that issue will be relevant, too. Tap on it.

Tap-along for self-blame:

Tap on the side of the hand point and say:

'Even though I have this illness, I deeply and completely accept myself, without judgment.'

'Even though I don't deserve to be ill, I accept myself with compassion. '

'Even though I don't want to be ill, I accept myself anyway.'

Then tap round the points.

Crown of the head: 'I'm doing the best I can.'

Eyebrow: 'I am not to blame.'

Side of the eye: 'I am human.'

Under the eye: 'Humans cannot be perfect.'

Under the nose: 'But I am perfectly human.'

Chin: 'I did not decide to be ill.'

Collarbone: 'I choose to discover how to be well.'

Underarm: 'I ask my unconscious mind to discover how to recover.'

Crown of the head: 'I am a work in progress.'

And then tap **round the rest of the points** just alternating these two phrases: 'I accept myself with compassion' and 'I am a work in progress'.

There are also things we can do to set and keep our bodies at an energy level that is least likely to make us vulnerable to illness and most likely to allow us to enjoy the swiftest recovery and the best health we can.

 Soraya had had chronic fatigue syndrome and was still recovering from it when she discovered EFT. She was no longer bed-ridden, as she had been when the illness was at its worst, but she still had days when she lacked the energy to do anything much at all.

Like many chronic fatigue sufferers, she was in a bind. She felt she needed to start to get back to exercise and to build up her stamina a little at a time. But if she did even slightly too much, she would be back in bed the next day. She was discouraged and angry about this lingering illness.

Soraya had done a lot of thinking. She recognized that when she became ill, she had been really driving herself. She had been stressed about work but was still driving herself relentlessly. Chronic Fatigue meant she just had to stop. Later she felt that the part of her that had stopped her had been really on her side. It had made her do what she was unwilling to do for herself. Not that it stopped her being really angry about it. But now she wondered what would have happened to her if she had kept driving herself so hard.

She had also had to move back in with her mother. This had been the last thing she wanted to do but she had no choice. She was unable to care for herself and could not afford to live alone. Living with her mother again brought her up against a lot of unresolved issues between the two of them. Soraya tapped on a lot of negative memories of times when her mother had not responded to her the way she had wanted. And she talked to her mother. They both came to understand better the other's take on many incidents both remembered. Their relationship became more warm and loving and supportive.

Soraya switched to using a different set-up phrase for a lot of her tapping. It was, 'I accept myself with compassion.'

Gradually, Soraya got back to her interrupted life. But as she did, there were big changes in her approach. First, she now had a strong and supportive alliance with her mother, rather than a lot of unfinished business and unresolved anger and resentment. She was less judgmental of herself, too, and she had learned that working herself so punishingly and relentlessly would not solve anything. It would just risk catapulting her into a black pit she wanted never to visit again.

Remember that there is a difference between being cured and being healed. Even if you can-not cure your condition, you may find that tapping helps you to heal. Healing is what we have when we are at peace with what we cannot change.

18. Pain relief

EFT can be a useful painkiller, without the risk of side-effects. If you have a headache or a pain in your hip, or an earache or a knee that throbs if you walk too far, EFT can beat a painkiller from a bottle.

Pain is a signal. It is a message from one part of the body to the brain that the brain interprets as pain. Sometimes it is telling us that we have overdone things physically, or that we are too stressed, or even that we are holding old injury or trauma in our bodies. EFT can be a useful pain-killer, without the risk of side effects. It can help you detach both from the physical sensation of pain, as well as the negative emotions attached to it. But sometimes pain is signalling something serious that needs to be diagnosed and treated. EFT is not a substitute for conventional medical diagnosis.

When you want to work with EFT with pain that you are feeling right now you need to:

- **Rate intensity.** Ask yourself on a scale of 1–10 how bad the pain is, where one is hardly detectable and ten is as bad as you can imagine.

- **Pinpoint** the location. Pinpoint it exactly. Not just 'my hip' but 'my left hip, just slightly to the front', or not just 'my leg' but 'the back of the calf of my right leg'.

- **Describe** it as specifically as you can. Is it hot, cold, throbbing or stabbing? Is it there all the time or does it come and go? Does it have a colour? Does it have a shape? Does it have a texture?

- **Word it.** Now work out a set-up statement like 'Even though I have this throbbing, hot orange pain just behind my left knee, I deeply and completely accept myself.'

- **Tap on it.** Tap on the side of the hand point saying that full sentence three times. Then take out a reminder phrase such as, in the example above, 'this throbbing, hot, orange pain just behind my left knee', and tap around the points from the top of the head to the underarm point, twice, repeating that phrase as you tap.

- **Rate again.** What number is it now?

- **Re-describe.** If the sensation has changed, change the words to describe it as it now is. If it has moved, change the description of the location. If the intensity has changed make a note of what it is now.

- **Reword the set-up** statement and start again.

- **Continue** until the pain is zero. Or until you have done it twice and haven't noticed any further change.

- If that happens, skip forward to 'The emotional component of pain' on page 112.

CASE STUDY

James was in his mid-seventies and had pain in both hips from arthritis. He was doing an EFT introductory course because he wanted to learn how to use EFT to control the pain better.

As he started a group exercise, he rated the pain in one hip as nine, while the pain in the other was seven. He gave an accurate description of the location and the sensation of the worse hip in his set-up phrase. When he had finished a couple of rounds, the pain in that hip had gone. But the pain in the other hip was exactly the same as it had been when he started. EFT had made a difference only where he had focussed on it. The other hip only reduced when he started again, with his attention focussed on it.

From that time onwards, whenever he felt pain in his hips he tapped to turn down the signal.

Chasing the pain

Sometimes when we start to tap on pain, it seems to move around the body. When it does, just follow it. It may lead you a bit of a dance around your body and eventually go down to zero. Job done. Bear in mind that the sensation might keep changing, so you'll need to change your words to match. So a burning sensation in your right knee might become a throbbing feeling in your right hip. But a few rounds later you might be dealing with a stabbing in the back of your ribs.

The emotional component of pain

Sometimes you will suddenly find that instead of a different physical sensation or a different location of the sensation, you have spontaneously accessed something emotional. When that happens, switch to the emotional issue. Equally, if you have reduced the pain but not completely got rid of it, and you do another round and the same still holds true, you should also switch to looking at the emotional component of pain. This means either:

> The feeling you have about having it

Or:

> The emotion you think might be causing it

It is easy enough to know what emotion we have about having pain but often we do not know, or do not know we know, what underlies it. But we can always guess. Usually if we really guess we are just letting our unconscious minds tell us something we don't consciously know.

Now, tap on the emotion about or underlying it and see if that makes the difference.

 Guessing is a great way to access information we have but don't know we do. It just puts us in touch with what we unconsciously know. Whenever you really do not know what number to put on a feeling or what might have kicked something off in your system, try just guessing. You may be surprised how well it can work.

The limits of EFT with pain – going deeper

EFT may reduce pain but not eliminate it completely for any one of several reasons:

If it is caused by some irreversible damage that has been done to the body. Studies of back pain have shown that the amount of pain people feel does not necessarily reflect the damage to their spines. However, structural damage may keep sending pain signals to the brain that will not switch off, or not switch off completely.

If there is some secondary gain to having the pain. You probably don't have to think to know what the downside of your pain is. But what is the upside? Sometimes, even without being consciously aware of it, we can be getting something out of having pain. For example, might you have to go back to an awful job, or spend less time with your loved ones if you were not in pain? Or is there a legal claim still to be settled related to the cause of the pain? If you're waiting to go to court to argue for compensation, for example, or waiting to settle an insurance claim, there may be a real conflict between the part of you that wants to be pain-free and the part that feels you deserve a maximum pay-out and that having pain may help you to secure it.

Sometimes just recognizing what the gain is will give you the information you need to deal with that in another way.

If the pain has a message. Is your pain trying to tell you something? The something could be that you need to have more time to relax, or that you need to go to your doctor for a diagnosis, or that you are in a relationship that is toxic for you, or that the friend who always leaves you feeling drained and exhausted is always taking, never giving and just not good for you. Ask the pain – and listen to what it says.

Ask yourself this: if the pain could write you a letter, what do you think it would say to you?

If the pain started with an accident or some other physically traumatic event. We experience physical trauma in our bodies and seem to tend to store it there. If you have pain that goes back to an accident, try to use EFT on the trauma memory first, and then check out the pain. Sometimes it goes completely, other times it reduces dramatically once you have dealt with the trauma.

Not only is the event often stored in the body but other emotions may be trapped with it. It may be that you are still angry with someone else who was involved. Or maybe you still blame yourself for what happened. Or are you furious with the way someone treated you afterwards?

Emotions like these may also be trapped in your system and experienced as physical pain. Clear them, and the pain will reduce – or often go completely.

Debbie volunteered at a workshop to do some tapping on the lower back pain that she had had for more than twenty years after a pony bolted and threw her into a wooden wall. She was an excellent rider and had broken bones before. But this time, when her body healed, she was left with a residue of pain that was constant if she sat for any length of time.

As tapping peeled away the layers, what emerged was that she felt she had deserved to be punished for being over-confident, arrogant even. Because there was still some damage, she also had a belief that she had to have some pain.

As she tapped, she began to reframe her views about the accident and herself. Had she been irresponsibly impulsive? Or had she simply been exuberant in the fearless way teenagers often are? Then she tapped on the belief that pain was inevitable and it melted away, too. At the end of the session her pain had gone from eight to zero.

---

19. Irritable Bowel Syndrome (IBS)

Irritable bowel syndrome, or IBS, is something of a 21st century scourge. It is the diagnosis doctors give to people who have some combination of abdominal pain, bloating and diarrhoea or constipation after they have ruled out other possible causes.

IBS is a problem with the way the bowel is functioning, not with its structure. What should happen is that food should move through the large bowel, a hollow tube surrounded by muscle, in a rhythmic wave pattern. But stress, whether physical or emotional, makes the muscles tense and go into spasm.

The jury is still out about how much it is a physical problem and how much it might be a psychological one. We know that for some people some foods are triggers while for others diet makes no difference. And we know that for people who have it, stress always makes it worse. Often it starts after something clearly physical – a stomach bug, a bad reaction to antibiotics, food poisoning. But it is a mystery why some people then just get over it and never give it another thought while for others it seems almost to take over their lives.

There may be a clue in the fact that we have neurons – brain cells – in our guts. The gut is actually one of three 'brains'. (Besides it and the one in our heads we have a 'brain' in our hearts. But that is another story.) In evolutionary terms, this 'brain' in the gut was actually the original one. It is the only 'brain' in really simple, primitive organisms. (Think slug.) Which makes sense when you think that no species is likely to survive long enough even to reproduce if it does not know when it needs to eat. To complicate matters, there is some evidence that sufferers have a more sensitive physiological gut reaction to emotional ups and downs than other people.

The trouble with having IBS is that it tends to create a vicious circle. People who have it are anxious that they will have it, and being anxious that they will makes it more likely, which makes them more anxious next time, which makes it more likely next time …

IF YOU REMEMBER ONE THING Don't self-diagnose IBS. Its symptoms can mimic those of other conditions which need medical intervention, so check it out with your doctor.

IBS STRATEGY

- Start with your beliefs. If you have any beliefs about what IBS is or about whether you can get over it, tap on them. For example, do you believe it's a condition that you will always have? Or do you believe it's entirely physical and stress makes no difference to it? Check out how true they feel and keep tapping until they no longer seem true.

- Tap on your memories of having IBS.

     Was there a time when a social event was completely ruined for you by your fear that you would have an accident? If there was, run the memory through your head and isolate the worst few minutes. Now pretend you have that memory on a DVD and do the Movie Technique.

     Was there a time or were there times when you actually had an accident? It is even more important that you clear any memories like these with the Movie Technique.

- Did yours start with food poisoning, or a stomach bug or a reaction to an antibiotic? If so, tap on that, too.

- Think back to when it started and recall whether there was some kind of specific stomach upset at the time or not, and if not, what else was going on in your life then? Were you particularly stressed? Had you just started a new job? Had a relationship ended?

     When you think back to that time, see what negative emotions are still in your system from whatever was troubling you then and tap to clear them. Are you still angry? Or afraid? Or humiliated? It will help to clear those feelings about then now.

- It will make you less susceptible if you clear some of the major stresses and past stressors from your life. Working through the chapters of this book on being your own therapist and on stress may help unravel some of the issues working alongside your IBS that are keeping you vulnerable.

- A high percentage of the people who have IBS also have anxiety. If that applies to you, work through the chapters on anxiety in this book.

- When you are anxious about going somewhere, tap on your fears to keep the anxiety level as low as you can before you go.

- When you are in a situation where you feel stressed and you feel it would make it worse if you tapped openly, just imagine you are. Or nip into the loo and give yourself a secret tapping top-up.

 Anna was a 30-year-old teacher and mother of two who was extremely anxious about going back to work after she had had three years off to be a full-time mother. As the date drew closer she thought more and more of a time before she became pregnant when she had frequent bouts of diarrhoea whenever there was anything particularly stressful to deal with.

If she had to go to a parents' meeting or there was an upcoming inspection, she spent more and more time in the lavatory. She became bloated. She had severe abdominal pain. Now the more she worried, the more she began to suffer her old IBS symptoms. She was beginning to dread being in front of a class of seven-year-olds again. Would she be a good teacher? Could she keep a class under control?

Social events became daunting ordeals to get through. What if she needed a lavatory urgently and could not find one? What if she lost control completely?

Anna got lucky. A friend told her about EFT and she started to tap every time she felt anxious. She tapped every time she felt any small warning signals from her gut. She tapped when she thought about going back into a classroom. She tapped and tapped and tapped.

Now, Anna was a perfectionist so she was not content just to try to banish her symptoms. She wanted to know why she had been vulnerable in this way. So she began to work through her Personal Peace Plan. As she worked through her memories, she had a sudden realization. She was so much of a perfectionist that she was putting herself under pressure in everything that she did.

Where did she learn that nothing less than perfect would be good enough? The answer was there, in the early memories she listed, in which she constantly got a steady drip of criticism from her mother. Nothing was ever quite good enough to please her. So Anna tried harder and harder and harder. She believed that if she could just do everything perfectly, her mother would approve of her.

Once Anna had cleared enough of those memories, she began to feel like a different person. She was more relaxed – in mind and body, and her IBS became a thing of the past.

20. EFT for eating and weight

Can EFT help me lose weight? Can it take away my bad eating habits? Can it boost my willpower?

The good news is that it can help. The bad news is that it will need an investment of time and effort from you. It cannot do it all by itself.

EFT isn't a magic weight loss formula. Nor is it an instant cure for disordered eating. But it can be a really helpful tool to get your eating and your size under your own control, if you are prepared to do the work with it.

 Disordered eating is eating that you know gets out of control at times – say when you are sad or bored or fed up – or eating that has got into really bad habits. But is not a full-on eating disorder. Anorexia nervosa – where people severely restrict their food intake, often to the point of starvation – is the psychiatric disorder with the highest mortality rate. It needs specialist skilled professional intervention. Don't try to self-treat anorexia. Bulimia – where people binge eat and then purge the food by vomiting – is a spectrum, but in more serious cases also needs skilled professional help.

It is a sad fact that so many people's lives are shadowed by how much they would really like to lose weight. And it is even sadder that most of them have already done it and then put it back on. What they want now is to lose it – again.

Eating and weight are complex and the potential underlying issues infinitely varied. If we want to stop smoking, we never need to have a cigarette again. If we want to control our eating, we still have to eat. We do not have the option of just going cold turkey.

It is also likely to be much more complicated psychologically. Our self-image, our sense of worth, our need to anaesthetize pain, banish boredom, stuff down anger or sadness or humiliation or fear can all be driving us to overeat. We may have got confusing early messages about eating and food and us.

We may, unconsciously, both yearn to be a certain size and shape and fear what we will have to deal with if we are. Or we may fear that if we succeed in becoming our ideal weight we will no longer have something to blame for our disappointments in love, our failure to get the job or the promotion we want. We will be left with nothing to hide behind.

Although those of us who want to lose weight have much in common, we are individuals. We have different goals and different obstacles trip us up. So you can get started by looking at your goals. Are they to do with behaviour? Is it what you eat that you aim to change? Or is it lack of exercise you want to tackle? Or both? Or why, when you start to make progress, you seem always to sabotage yourself?

Begin by thinking what your personal goals are. Which of these do you want to deal with?

- Eating
- Exercise
- Cravings
- Beliefs
- Body image
- Emotions that drive you to eat
- Whatever it is that you get from staying as you are

 Make a note of your goals so you can come back to them from time to time to see if you have achieved them, or if they have changed.

The physiology of fat

Studies of identical twins suggest that the urge to binge may be to some extent genetic. That doesn't mean, however, that we don't have a choice whether we do it or not. It just means some people are more likely to crave more than others. You still have the last word about you. You get to choose for yourself.

Being hard-wired to crave would once have made sense for our survival – otherwise we might have been reluctant to go out of the nice safe, warm cave to hunt. And, since hunting was a hit-and-miss affair, wouldn't it have made sense to eat as much as we could when we had food? And might natural selection not have favoured the people who were best at storing excess eating as fat?

Of course today, with high calorie foods available all the time and everywhere, that ceases to an advantage and becomes a potential minefield. Are our brains, with the best of intentions, trying to trick us into eating more?

 Tap a few rounds on this to set the internal context for getting on top of your eating. It is good to go back to from time to time, just for a few minutes each time. It is really addressing your unconscious rather than your conscious mind. Tap on the side of the hand point while you say: 'Even though there is a part of me that is trying to trick me into eating for my own good, I deeply and completely accept myself.' And then: 'Even though I know it is a trick, it is doing it for my own good, and I deeply and completely accept myself. And then: 'Even though that part of me is really trying to trick me to help me, I thank it for its intention, and I deeply and completely accept all the parts of myself.'

Then tap around the points a couple of times with these reminder phrases:

Crown of the head: 'Some part of me is trying to tell me it's good to eat sugar.'

Eyebrow: 'I thank it for its intention.'

Side of the eye: 'I know it really wants to help. I thank it for its intention.'

Under the eye: 'I don't need to store fat.'

Under the nose: 'I have plenty of food.'

Chin: 'I don't need to eat when I'm not really hungry.'

Collarbone: 'I don't need to store fat.'

Underarm: 'There is plenty of good nourishing food for me.'

Crown of the head: 'I want to ask the part of me that is trying to tell me to eat sugar to find a different way to help me.'

Eyebrow: 'I know that part of me is on my side.'

Side of the eye: 'I want to ask it to have a different role.'

Under the eye: 'To help me in a different way.'

Under the nose: 'I know that part of me can be really creative.'

Chin: 'I want it to use its creativity to help me in a different way.'

Collarbone: 'I thank this part of me for its intention.'

Underarm: 'I want that part of me to know there is plenty of good food whenever I need it.'

Stress and weight

Many of us respond to stress by eating too much. But that is only half the story. We also now understand that stress causes us to overproduce cortisol which is related to abdominal fat and makes it more difficult for us to lose weight. It also interferes with nutrient absorption so that even if we are eating well we may not be nourished well.

So if you know you have high stress levels and you want to lose weight, use what is relevant in this chapter but also have a look at the chapter on EFT and Stress. The more you reduce your stress, the more easily you will get your eating and weight under your own control.

The neurology of fat

When we overeat, especially sugar and other carbohydrates that produce sugar, the same part of the brain lights up as if we are taking recreational drugs. People who are obese and 'addicted' to food have only to see, smell or think about these foods to stimulate the production of dopamine, just as some drugs do. Dopamine has different functions in different parts of the brain. It can promote motivation, improve mood, and provide reward and gratification. When we get a sugar hit we also release serotonin into the brain. Increasing levels of it is one of the ways doctors treat depression. Its roles include regulating mood, appetite, and sleep.

It obviously makes sense to have another way – like EFT – to take control of our emotional regulation so we will have less perception of need to use food as our drug of choice to do it. We can use EFT in all the ways already outlined in this book to deal directly with negative emotions when we know what they are. But our systems are clever at being sneaky. It's easy for our bodies to decide not to feel the feeling at all, and to block it by craving something that can anaesthetize those emotions.

When this is what is going on, what we need is some tapping techniques – like the two that follow – to help us banish the craving. The first is a good way to loosen the hold over us that some particular food always or often has. Set it up when you have time to do it. If it wears off in time, just do it again. The second is an in-the-moment response to the urge to stuff ourselves with whatever is available at that moment.

Quelling a craving

Many people, when they try to get control of what they eat and lose some weight, find that craving one particular food is what regularly trips them up. Often the same food was responsible for much of the weight they need to lose in the first place. It might be crisps for one person or chocolate for another or biscuits or cheese. If this is you, here is a good way to use tapping to turn off or down the intensity of that habitual craving.

Get yourself some of what it is that you habitually crave – crisps, chocolate, cake, fresh bread, biscuits, wine or whatever it is – and sit down with it. Notice everything about it.

- What does it look like?
- What does it smell like?
- What does it sound like?
- What do you think when you look at it?
- What does it taste like?
- What do you think about it?

Tap on everything about it that you can think of. Put all your thoughts and feelings, one at a time, into an EFT set-up and tap on them. So it might be, 'Even though I can smell that sweet, rich chocolate smell in my nose and the pit of my stomach, I deeply and completely accept myself.' Or it might be, 'Even though I can imagine the smooth, velvety, thick feeling of that chocolate in my mouth …', or 'Even though I can smell it and taste it just thinking about it …'.

When new thoughts come up, tap on them. Keep tapping until you find you feel quite differently about it. It may be that you no longer want it at all. Or it may be that you could still eat it but you no longer feel you could not do without it. You don't need to end up hating it. You just want to reduce its power to seduce you to a point where you have a choice. Once you have, you are back in control.

If, at any time, you feel it is starting to try to tyrannize you again, just repeat the exercise.

Quick craving killer

Here is another tapping option to use when you want to resist the urge to eat when you know you are not actually hungry, or to enable yourself to make a sensible choice with your head when you are hungry and you are deciding what to eat.

- When you feel the craving, focus on it to notice exactly what you feel and where in your body you feel it. Is it in the pit of your stomach, for example? Or your throat?

- Rate it on a scale of 1–10.

For this you do not use words.

- Just really concentrate on the feeling and its location.

- As you do, tap the collarbone point ten times.

- Still focussing on the craving, tap the under eye point ten times.

- Return to the collarbone and tap ten times.

Now find the gamut point. To locate it, make a fist – the gamut point is the dip on the back of your hand between the knuckles of the little finger and ring finger. Tap on it while you do the following:

- Close your eyes

- Open them

- Look down hard right (keeping your head steady, just moving your eyes)

- Look down hard left

- Roll your eyes round in one direction

- Roll them in the other

- Hum a few bars of music

- Count to five

- Hum a few more bars.

Now rate the craving again. If it is not yet zero, repeat until it is.

This is a brain balancing exercise borrowed from TFT. It uses bilateral stimulation, which means it involves using both sides of the brain in the processing, and it's amazingly effective at banishing a craving.

Jennifer's downfall was bread. She would come home from work and start eating it, with lashings of butter and a little jam, as she cooked the dinner for the rest of the family. Then she had dinner. And sometime she rounded off the evening with a little more bread before bed.

She could not work out exactly why she was doing it, but said she had a sense of being really empty, and of her life being really empty, and wanting somehow to fill it up. She started to use the quick craving killer the minute she started to feel the urge to eat bread.

There were setbacks. Sometimes she wanted the bread more than she wanted to not want it. But she persisted. Tapping on the craving had given her a way to be in control. Gradually she was able to manage the habit. The more often she won the battle, the more empowered she felt to fight back, and her weight started to go down.

Going deeper

So far we have been looking at some quick techniques to help you get on top of your particular difficulties with eating. But you may recognize that for really lasting results you need to go deeper. Doing some detective work on yourself might have a built-in bonus. You may have insights that enable you to deal with some of that emotional debris you have been carrying without knowing what it is or where it came from. If that happens, you may gain more than just progress towards the body you want to have. You may find yourself changing how you experience your life.

Some questions to ask yourself:

- How long have I been overeating?

- What else was going on in my life at the time I started?

- When do I overeat?

- Who else in my family is overweight?

- What happened last time I got to the weight I want to be?

- If I have feelings I wanted to stuff down what might they be?

- If there is some emptiness in my life, what might that be about?

- How would I spend the time I spend thinking about food if I did not have this obsession with it?

- What is the upside of being the weight I am?

- What is the downside?

- What is the upside of losing weight?

- What is the downside of losing weight?

- What is the upside of eating the way I do?

- What is the downside?

- What emotions am I trying to tranquilize?

- What do I think I would feel if I gave up eating the way I do? It might be:
  - Deprivation
  - Loss
  - Guilt
  - Anxiety
  - Emptiness
  - Fear

- How do I feel about myself at the weight I am?

- Who would I be if I did not eat the way I do?

- Who would I be if I were at my goal weight?

- How will my partner respond to me
  a) eating less?
  b) being lighter?

- How will my family respond to a) and b) as above?

- How will my friends respond to a) and b) as above?

- Who will be pleased if I succeed in this?

- Who will be displeased if I succeed in this?

- Who will pretend to be pleased but probably won't be?

Mary had lost weight several times before. Each time she did, it was only a matter of a short time before she put it back. Almost as soon as she stopped the strict eating plan she had devised for herself, she began to pile the pounds back.

When she tapped on her memories of each time this had happened, and her feelings about the fact that it had, she had a sudden realization. Every time she got to her ideal weight, her husband, Jonathan, began to be suspicious about where she went and who she saw. He would phone and text endlessly when she was out. He would put pressure on her to come home early.

He thought she was attractive to other men in a way that he did not think she was when she was overweight. Unconsciously, she responded to his pressure by putting the weight on and so stopping his unwanted behaviour. At some level, being overweight was less unpleasant for her than putting up with his possessive jealousy.

When she realized this, she tapped first on her feelings about his behaviour. Then, when she was feeling less emotional about it, she sat down with him and discussed it with him. Jonathan had not really been aware of what he was doing. Together, they were able to work out a plan to enable her to lose weight again, and this time to keep it off.

Some of the questions above may help you to understand why you have had trouble losing weight without even realizing it. Others may reveal directions you need to take your tapping. Still others may enable you to deal, in advance, with the way others are likely to respond to you.

So, for example, if you started to overeat at the time something stressful or painful or challenging was going on in your life, do you need to deal with whatever it was in another way so you can stop using eating to deal with it? What do you need to tap on to do this? The memory? The residual emotion?

Some of the questions may open your eyes to secondary gain – the advantages of having a problem – that you did not realize you were getting from it. Many problems have an upside as well as a downside, but we often do not consciously realize what it is.

Secondary gain means there is potential secondary loss. Lose weight and what else will go out of your life with it? If you decided to have a really sensible eating regime, would it mean that you could not meet the friends with whom you have coffee and chocolate cake on a Saturday morning? Or could you still go but make yourself an outsider by not having chocolate cake? Such unconsidered side-effects can have more unconscious effect on us than we realize until we take them out in the light and look at them. Often once we do they no longer influence us.

Or, if you uncover a belief you did not realize you had, you can tap on it. Say you find you think that, because everyone in your family is fat, you have no choice but to be too. Your head might tell you that this is because you all shared the same dysfunctional eating patterns. But it might not *feel* true. Ask yourself on a scale of 1–10 how true it feels.

Then tap on something like, 'Even though I don't believe I can lose weight because everyone in my family is fat, I deeply and completely accept myself.' Check in with yourself to discover how true that belief feels afterwards. Keep repeating until you know it no longer determines what is possible for you.

Metabolism

When you cut down your food intake, especially if you do it too drastically, your body will think there is a famine and will try to help out by conserving as much fat as it can for you. Farmers fattening cattle for slaughter know this. They cut rations for a bit and then beef them right up so they get a maximum weight – and price – when the cattle are weighed in at the abattoir.

People who have done a lot of crash dieting, or alternating bingeing and semi-starving over the years, may have really confused their metabolic rate – the rate at which the body burns food or stored fat for energy.

Some practical ways to increase your metabolism include eating breakfast, increasing your water intake, doing aerobic exercise, building muscle, reducing stress, getting enough sleep, eating healthily including healthy snacks between meals, and being consistent about how much and when you eat.

At another level we unconsciously set our metabolic rate in response to our perception of the environment. That is why, if you have been on diet after diet, you probably have an unhelpfully low metabolic rate. Women with a history of dieting will often say they have only to look at a chocolate wrapper to put on weight! Their unconscious minds think there is always famine where they are, and will be trying to help to keep them alive on as little food as possible.

It helps if you can convince your unconscious mind that there is plenty of food and you do not need to be storing as much as you possibly can as fat. The tap-along below is a way of combining tapping with talking to your unconscious mind to update it and give it more accurate information on what your real needs are.

TRY IT NOW!

Tapping for your metabolism
On the side of the hand point:

'Even though my body is running slow, I deeply and completely accept myself.

'Even though I know it's running slowly because it wants to protect me, I deeply and completely accept myself.

'Even though I know my metabolism is running below its maximum, I accept all of myself including my body anyway.'

Crown of the head: 'I am running slow.'

Eyebrow: 'My metabolism has slowed right down.'

Side of the eye: 'I have plenty to eat.'

Under the eye: 'I have all the nourishment I need when I need it.'

Under the nose: 'I know the system controlling my metabolism is trying to help me.'

Chin: 'I know it's trying to protect me.'

Collarbone: 'I thank it for that intention.'

Underarm: 'But I want it to know I have plenty of nourishment.'

Crown of the head: 'There is plenty of food.'

Eyebrow: 'I am not at risk of starving.'

Side of the eye: 'I am asking my metabolism to speed up to a healthy rate.'

Under the eye: 'It's safe for my metabolism to speed up now.'

Under the nose: 'I am asking my metabolism to speed up.'

Chin: 'There is no famine.'

Collarbone: 'I am asking my metabolism to go to its highest healthy rate.'

Underarm: 'I am really safe now.'

 Words for tapping sequences are only suggestions. It is strongly recommended that you use them only for ideas and that you change them, as far as you can, for words that are more relevant or resonate more for you.

---

21. Stopping smoking

Many smokers consider themselves experts at giving it up. They have done it – again and again and again. But just mention stopping once more and they get a sinking failure feeling. It reminds them that every attempt just ended up being one more flop.

Others have never tried because they just don't believe they can. The health statistics scare them. They are noticing how their stamina has slumped. They cannot hide from themselves how they puff when they try to keep up with non-smoking friends. But they just don't believe it's possible to give up. Better to put up a mental smokescreen to hide behind and tell themselves about that 100-year-old woman they have heard about who has smoked 30 a day since the age of 15 …

The good news is that it *is* possible to stop. The better news is that every time you tried and failed in the past you learned something. Unconsciously, you have been building up a resource bank with everything you need to know to succeed. And the best news is that it might not be as bad as you think. Some people don't even have withdrawal symptoms. But those who do can use tapping to zap them.

If you have been a habitual long-term smoker you may feel that a cigarette is your friend. Some friend, since it is probably robbing you of years of your life! But when we are stressed, bored or busy it is difficult for us not to fall back on the old habitual way we have of finding relief. And for a smoker, that means smoking.

Do you tell yourself you enjoy smoking? Just sit back for a minute and check. How many cigarettes a day do you actually really enjoy? Most people, when they reflect honestly about this, recognize that it is only one or two a day that are a positive pleasure. They may be spending a lot of money and doing a lot of damage to their health for a quite small return.

Smokers often say they experience smoking as relaxing. It is not. Taking a break to have it may be. Satisfying, temporarily, the craving for nicotine may feel as if it is. But all it really relaxes is the physical craving. Nicotine is a stimulant. It hypes us up. It turns on a happy switch to release substances including feel-good dopamine. Half an hour or so later that switches off again. The buzz is short-lived. The damage to our health is not.

Stopping smoking does not mean saying goodbye to dopamine. There are other ways you can persuade your brain to produce more. One of them is exercise which is brilliant for anyone putting smoking behind them. Stick at it for a few days and it will start to give you a buzz. And that is just what you need as you make the transition from smoker to smoke-free.

As the smoke-free days go by exercise will become easier. And it will increase your metabolic rate. Putting on weight when you stop smoking is not inevitable. If you up your exercise regime and make sure you do not fall into the trap of substituting food (especially cakes, biscuits, and sweets) for cigarettes you can stop smoking without piling on the pounds.

Nicotine is not alone. There are more than 4000 chemicals in cigarettes. Some are toxic. Some are known to cause cancer. Thirty per cent of cancer deaths can be attributed to smoking. This does not just mean lung cancer. Smoking increases the risk of cervical, pancreatic, bladder, stomach, kidney, liver, mouth, lip and throat cancer and leukaemia.

STOPPING SMOKING STRATEGIES

Start with beliefs

What are your beliefs about stopping smoking? Check how true each belief that might get in your way *feels*. If you find it difficult to access the strength of feeling of the belief try saying it out loud. For example, it might be, 'I cannot stop smoking'. When you say it, see how your body responds. On each belief that you identify or that resonates with you from the list of suggestions below, tap on: 'Even though I have this belief (say what it is) I accept myself anyway.' Check to see how much it has reduced. If it is not gone or going, repeat.

- Do you believe you cannot stop?

- Do you believe you can stop but you will start again?

- Do you believe it has to be really difficult?

- Do you believe you do not know how to mix with people if you do not have a cigarette to shelter behind?

- Do you believe it is inevitable that you will put on weight if you stop?

Next, look at your feelings. Imagine yourself as a non-smoker. Try to picture yourself in all the situations in which you smoke now but not smoking. See what comes up for you.

- Do you feel twitchy?

- Do you feel scared?

- Do you feel angry?

- Do you feel this is not really you?

- Do you feel anxious that you will not belong in the group of your smoking buddies?

- Do you feel you will not know who you really are anymore?

Tap on whatever feelings arise until you can picture that situation again and not get them.

Rehearse

Mentally, work your way through a non-smoking day. When do you usually have your first cigarette? Would you go for a morning cigarette break at work? Think of practical strategies as you imagine your way through. For example, if you always have a cigarette as soon as you finish dinner then maybe you could load the dishwasher or put on a load of washing instead.

As you do this practical mental preparation, notice what emotions or beliefs come up. Make a note of them. When you get to the end of the day in your head, tap on whatever came up.

Go through the day again. Keep going back until you can imagine it all, without feeling anything negative.

The inner war

It is not unusual for people to have an inner conflict when they think about stopping smoking. They know that one part of them wants to stop and one does not. The part that does not may have a dozen different reasons for not going along with what the rest of the system wants.

Tap on any of these that resonate with you, or that you can uncover as relevant for you:

- 'Even though part of me wants to stop smoking and part of me really doesn't …'

- 'Even though maybe part of me thinks I don't deserve to stop smoking …'

- 'Even though part of me thinks I will never get going in the mornings without a cigarette …'

- 'Even though part of me thinks I will have nothing that is just for me if I don't smoke …'

- 'Even though part of me thinks I will not have any of the rebel left in me …'

- 'Even though part of me doesn't want to risk failing again …'

Killing cravings

This is absolutely key to success. As with food, you can use tapping to kill any cravings that come up. I am using 'cravings' here as a word that covers a multitude of different feelings. For some people this pressing, almost irresistible, desire to have a cigarette might come as a queasy feeling in the stomach, or a hyped up feeling all over, or a mouth sensation, or a thought that won't go away. There are a hundred different varieties.

Tapping away craving, however you experience it, is most efficient if you really notice in detail what you feel and where you feel it and describe it to yourself in accurate detail. That way your attention will really be on your experience. Where is it? Does it have a shape? Does it have a colour? Exactly what is it that you feel?

So for example, your words might be, 'Even though I have this dull grey thudding in my left temple …'. Make sure you rate your subjective perception of how strong the craving is before and after, and be persistent. It may take time to quell the craving completely.

146

Emergency measures

- If you need a really quick craving killer, remember the anxiety stopping point. Just thump your chest, quite hard, about where men knot their ties.

- If you are somewhere you would be uncomfortable to be seen tapping, remember you can imagine that you are tapping. Really put your attention on it, and imagine each point in turn.

- Use 'your point'. If you have found that one point seems more powerful for you, then use just that in an emergency

- Tap without words. If you are feeling a really strong urge to buy a packet of cigarettes or to light one right this minute, don't worry about the words. Just tap and tap and tap until the intensity is less compelling. Then you can go back to describing it in detail to finish the job of getting rid of the residual desire.

One of the commonest reasons that people stop smoking for a few days and then take it up again is alcohol. There is often a habitual association between drinking and smoking. But even more powerfully, alcohol disinhibits. So many people go to a bar determined not to smoke and a few drinks into the evening say to themselves, 'Just one won't hurt.' The morning after they may or may not have a hangover but odds are they will be battling tobacco again. Consider making it easy on yourself by drinking something non-alcoholic for the first week or two.

Carry on tapping

Don't stop tapping too soon. Even when you are confident that you're now a confirmed ex-smoker, a bit of daily tapping will keep the possibility of relapse at bay. Whatever feelings or emotions come up, whether or not they seem smoking-related, tap on them. Without your habitual smokescreen, you may access feelings you were trying to hide from yourself.

Remember, too, that EFT makes a great new coping strategy for situations of stress, boredom, nervousness or feeling overwhelmed in which you once would have turned to a cigarette for solace. It will ensure you no longer need to.

Last word

Don't think of giving up as a negative. Many people make stopping the start of a whole new lifestyle. They welcome the cough most ex-smokers get for a few weeks while their lungs are cleaning and clearing themselves out as a sign of regeneration. They love it when they notice they are thinking more clearly, now that nicotine is no longer constricting their capillaries and they are getting a better blood supply to the brain. They love it that they are sleeping better. So they decide on a healthier diet. They schedule regular exercise. The better they feel the more they look after themselves.

Down the line they look back not at when something went out of their lives but as when a whole new healthy life began.

 John was a 45-year-old man who had been smoking since he was sixteen. He started because all his friends did. He wanted to be part of the group. Now they had all given up but he couldn't. So cigarettes were no longer filling the same 'belonging' role in his life as they had. They were doing exactly the opposite.

He had tried to give up three times before. The first time, he thought he was going to be made redundant and the stress got to him. Without even thinking, he turned to his old support system. Before he realized, he was a smoker again. The second time he was more on guard. He was determined not to slip again. And he did not, until one very boozy evening when he thought it would be safe now to have 'just one'. It turned out to be the start of a slippery slope.

This was his third time and he really wasn't even getting started. He would be cigarette-free for a day and then he would relapse again. When he stopped, a lot of emotions came up. He could not quite pin down what they were. But they seemed to be a cocktail of sadness and anxiety and he was not sure what else.

He hated smoking now. It was no longer his ticket to acceptance by his friends. It had become just the great excluder. He was the one going outside on his own to have a cigarette. It was taking his money. It was taking his health. So why was he so deeply sad at the thought of giving up?

He started tapping on all these feelings. The sadness particularly puzzled him. He tapped and tapped on the sadness. He closed his eyes and let his mind drift back to when he might have felt sadness like that before. Then, out of the blue, he got it. He flashed back to an evening in the pub, when he and his father were having a pint and a cigarette together. It was how and where they had built a new relationship as adult to adult.

His father had died a few months earlier. There was some unconscious part of him that felt that if he stopped smoking, he was breaking that final link between them. It seemed somehow disloyal. Consciously, he knew this was not true. But at another level …

Once he realized and acknowledged that, he was on the way to his final successful campaign. He tapped on a lot of feelings about the loss of his father. Gradually the sadness gave way to happy memories of the bond they had shared. And with that unrecognized barrier out of the way, he had his last puff.

John is now an ex-smoker.

22. Stress

Stress is what we call it when we do not have enough resources – or think we don't – to handle the mental and physical demands life throws at us. We have too much to fit into a day. We have too many roles making their demands on us. Some of them are beyond our control. We may know at work that some jobs are going to be axed as the company tightens its belt. But we don't get to decide who stays and who goes. It might feel the only way we can influence the outcome is to work harder and longer than anyone else. So we add the stress of overwork to the stress of feeling insecure about work.

Of course, we need a certain amount of stress to give us the oomph to get up in the morning. Stress can motivate us to make changes and explore new possibilities. But too much is toxic for mind and body. It clouds thought, impairs memory and interferes with our ability to fight off illness. We stop sleeping well. Our immune systems gear down, or even crash. We stop enjoying sex. When we are too stressed we find we keep catching everything that is going around. We are more at risk of heart disease, high blood pressure, stroke, diabetes, asthma, ulcers.

Women suffering stress may have menstrual disorders, premenstrual tension and failure to ovulate. Men risk stress-related impotence. Three out of four of the complaints that take us to the doctor are stress-related. Stress costs the economy billions and billions of pounds a year.

Long-running stress makes it difficult for us to get on with other people – and with ourselves. And worst of all, if we are constantly stressed we not only have trouble turning off the production of stress hormones in our bodies but we actually become addicted to them. We can find we don't feel 'right' unless we are really stressed. That is why some people with really stressful working weeks go thrill-seeking at the weekend. Some of the other symptoms of stress may include:

- Tightness, discomfort or even pain in the chest

- Rapid or pounding heartbeat

- Dizziness/fainting/ feeling faint

- Difficulty sleeping/disturbed sleep/sleeping too much/ feeling unrefreshed after sleep

- Chronic tiredness/lack of energy

- Stomach upsets/indigestion/irritable bowel/stomach pain/nausea

- Dry mouth/a choking feeling/difficulty swallowing

- Sweaty palms

- Teeth grinding/clenched jaws

- Tremors and twitches

- Headaches

- Loss of appetite or overeating

- Rashes, skin problems

- Muscle aches and tension

- Frequent urination

- Breathlessness/hyperventilation (very fast, shallow breathing)

- Disturbed vision

- Drinking and/or smoking too much

- Nervousness/anxiety

- Mood swings/irritability

- Difficulty concentrating

 Some of these stress symptoms can also be symptoms of other health problems that you may need to check out with your doctor.

STRESS STRATEGY

If you think back to the definition of stress at the start of this chapter, part of the equation is what resources we have available to deal with the demands facing us. When you use this book to teach yourself how to use EFT you already have one more resource than you had before. You have taken the first anti-stress step. To move forward, try some of the following strategies.

First aid

To stop 'normal' stress tipping over into destructive stress, try the following:

- When you do feel stressed, tapping is a brilliant way to relax. Just describe to yourself what you are feeling and put it into an EFT set-up statement.

- Sometimes it helps to do it this way: close your eyes and take a minute or two to really notice what is going on for you. Just notice, without judging or analysing. What takes your attention? Is it a thought? Is it a physical sensation? Is it an emotion? Whatever it is, tap on it, still without judgment.

So it might be something like: 'Even though I have this feeling that I just cannot cope, I deeply and completely accept myself.' Or: 'Even though I feel I cannot concentrate, I accept myself anyway.' Or: 'Even though I feel this fluttering anxiety in my stomach, I accept myself completely.' Or: 'Even though I have this fast shallow breathing and I feel dizzy I accept myself without judgement.' Or any one of a thousand other variations.

Stress management

- One good stress management strategy that takes only a few minutes a few times a day is to stop what you are doing, Take a minute or two to close your eyes and check in with yourself as above. Notice, as described above, just what is going on for you and tap on anything that is weighing on your mind or worrying you. Don't judge or try to work out why you feel as you do. Just accept it and tap on it.

This will help to prevent a build-up of stress. Over time, it may even establish a new default stress setting for yourself.

Stress-proofing

Divide and conquer. If you want to make your life as stress-proof as you can, the first step is to make a list of things you're stressed about. Cover all areas of your life – work, family, friendships, health. Now divide the list into what you can change and what you cannot.

- What you can change, change.

Sounds easy, doesn't it? But change rarely is. In theory it may, for example, be a no-brainer that you could easily schedule into your week a bit of time to do something you really enjoy. Time to smell the roses, or read a book or do whatever you feel like doing for no reason except that you like doing it.

But when you try you may find you run up against all manner of internal difficulties here. Say, for example, that when you really think about your life you realize that you put your partner, your children, your wider family, your friends, work, the local scout group – everyone you know – before yourself. You may realize you are right at the end of the queue.

When that penny drops, you may want to make some changes. But then you might start wondering would you be selfish if you showed yourself some consideration? If you wanted to work out a way to have something in your life that was just for you would other people like you less? Disapprove? Would you disapprove? Do you even believe it's possible?

- When you have worked out what blocking beliefs are getting in your way, tap on them. They might be things like:

'Even though I would be really selfish if I took some time for myself, I accept myself anyway.'

'Even though I don't believe it is possible to do less than I do, I accept myself.'

'Even though I don't know who I would be if I took my foot of the accelerator, I accept myself without judgement.'

'Even though I don't think I would be doing the right thing if I took some time off, I accept myself unconditionally anyway.'

Once you have changed the belief you may find it much easier than you thought to change the behaviour.

- You might even discover an unexpected bonus. Sometimes tapping on such a belief suddenly brings into awareness some past experience that was powerful in instilling that belief. EFT has a way of doing that. And it also offers tools to disempower the decision we made or the belief we took on board as absolute truth at that time.

This is an opportunity to go back to that memory and disempower it. Imagine you have it on a DVD and tap on it, using the Movie Technique.

- What you can't change …

Inevitably there are things in our lives that we cannot change. However, usually we can reduce the stress they produce in us just by changing the way we react to them. The circumstances may be outside our control but our response to them is ours to choose.

Let's say, for example, that your boss is demanding. She micromanages to a point that feels to you just short of bullying. She makes you feel that she does not think you have a brain of your own at all. As you hear that particular tone in her voice you start to feel like a school pupil again.

Close your eyes now and imagine that voice and let the feelings it provokes in you come up in your body. Now just let your mind drift back to a time when you have had that feeling before. Don't try. Just allow. When you remember, note it down. Keep your eyes closed and see if you can drift back to an even earlier time. Note that, too. Now tap on the memories that you have accessed, using the Movie Technique.

Typically, what really stresses us does so because it unconsciously reminds us of things we have found stressful or hurtful or harmful in the past. Clear the past and the present will change itself. You may still have a micromanaging boss who doesn't give you space to do the best job you could if she was not always in your face. But you will find you stress less about it.

What if it is an inside job?
Stress is not just a response to external circumstances. It can also be something we do to ourselves. If someone is constantly telling himself that nothing he does is good enough, or she is not good enough, or he has to be perfect to be good enough, or she is unlovable ... these and all their variations are a recipe for stress, however much or however little is actually going on in their lives. Put them alone on a desert island and they would be stressed.

The key here is self-acceptance. Self-acceptance is a central part of the EFT philosophy. When we tap we say, 'Even though … I accept myself' or some variation of that. But do we just do it on auto-pilot?

- Try saying it as if you mean it, even if you don't.

- Use variations like 'I accept myself anyway', or 'I accept myself without judgement', or 'I accept myself with compassion'.

- Do rounds of tapping using 'I accept myself' instead of the negative reminder phrase from set-up as you go round the points from the top of the head to the underarm point. Notice anything that comes up as you do. It may be a good clue to where you need to go next.

- Do your Personal Peace Plan, and see if you can't make friends with your inner critic.

 Jane was a 35-year-old married mother of two with a demanding full-time practice as an accountant. She did a lot to help her elderly parents, was on the board of governors at her daughters' school, arranged her working days around collecting her daughters from school, and taking them to swimming and ballet lessons. Often she kept on top of her work by doing it late at night. She prided herself

on doing everything in her work, relationship, partner, daughter, mother roles as well as she possibly could.

Friends thought she was amazing the way she kept all these balls in the air, seemingly effortlessly. Deep down, she felt she was not good enough and would soon be found out. Her survival strategy was to try harder, do more, set herself even more exacting standards.

Jane began to realize how stressed she was. She was sleeping badly. She exploded into anger easily. She was catching every virus that was going around. Life had become a black-and-white grind of getting through each day. There were many ticks on her daily 'to do' list. But there was no joy.

One of the first questions Jane addressed was why she was setting herself such cripplingly high standards. She had never got the concept of 'good enough'. She began to look at the difference between trying to do things well and feeling a failure if anything was less than perfect. Where did this unrealistic standard come from? She quickly realized that when she was a little girl her father had been impossible to please. However well she did at school, he had always expected her to do better. Bringing home school reports was an ordeal. Sometimes she would hide them for days. No matter how good her reports were, he never praised. He always just wanted to know why she had not done better. So next term, she would try even harder.

As she tapped on her feelings about this, she began to have insights. She had felt she was not good enough to please him. Now she began to see that he was impossible to please. All her life, long after she thought she had escaped his influence, there was a part of her that was still trying to be good enough to please him.

Now when she cleaned his kitchen for him, or cooked him a meal, or did his laundry, it was still never quite good enough. And every time he showed his displeasure, that inner 'I am not good enough' part of her was being reinforced.

Jane went back to a number of specific memories from that constant steady drip of disapproval and cleared the emotional residue from them using the Movie Technique. She started to feel more positive about herself. She took a few minutes out a few times a day to sit back and notice what she was feeling and tap on it. As she did, she used phrases like, 'I accept myself without judgment' and 'I accept myself unconditionally' and 'I accept myself even though I am not perfect and never can be.'

Now she was in a virtuous circle. She tapped when she felt stressed. And the less stress she felt the more efficiently and effortlessly she got through what she had to do each day. And now when her father criticized her, she really thought he was just a bad-tempered old man who did not know how to give praise. The less she judged herself, the more life began to flow.

Her final gift to herself was to realize how much she had put everyone – husband, children, parents, clients – before herself. She was almost missing from her own story. That was when she decided to schedule something every week just for herself. One week it might be a relaxing massage. Another it might be a walk in the park. Or coffee and cake with a friend. Or even a girls' night out in a wine bar. Jane was having a life again.

---

23. Insomnia

If you have trouble sleeping, tapping can help. Insomnia comes in many guises. Some people have trouble getting to sleep. Others go out like a light but have difficulty staying asleep. Yet others sleep well most nights and then, once in a while, it is as if they have forgotten where the off switch is. The way in which EFT will be most useful to you will depend partly on which category you fit into. Tailor your tapping to your experience.

 Start with the practical. Are you doing things that make good sleep more difficult?

- Do you drink too much coffee or coke or too much too late in the day? Caffeine and sleep are not good bedfellows. Experiment with cutting down. The same applies with alcohol, which can trick us by helping us get to sleep but then messing up a normal healthy sleep cycle so we wake too soon again or, when we do wake, we feel unrefreshed.

- Do you have wind-down time? If you watch anything too exciting on television or work on your computer until the last possible minute, your brain may just not know it's time to close down. Do something relaxing – perhaps reading, or a hot bath before you try to sleep.

- Cut down the possible stimulation in your bedroom. Turn off your phone. Leave your iPad at the door. Resist television. Don't read a gripping thriller.

Insomnia can be a symptom of many different emotional problems. Some people find that when they clear a lot of what is troubling them with EFT, better sleep happens by itself. You should also check in with yourself as to whether you are sleeping badly because you are stressed. If you are, work through the stress chapter of this book as well.

If you know you have trouble getting to sleep because you have had some bad nights, and you worry about whether this will be another, then tap on that before you go to bed.

It might be something like this:

On the side of the hand:

'Even though I have trouble sleeping, I accept myself.'

'Even though I just watch the clock moving on and I know I will feel terrible tomorrow, I accept myself.'

'Even though I am afraid this will be another bad night, I accept myself anyway.'

And then round the points with something along the lines of:

Crown of the head: 'I'm afraid of having another bad night.'

Eyebrow: 'I will feel terrible tomorrow.'

Side of the eye: 'I just cannot sleep.'

Under the eye: 'I will get to sleep just in time to get up.'

Under the nose: 'I cannot sleep.'

Chin: 'Things just go round and round in my head.'

Collarbone: 'I am so overtired I will never get to sleep.'

Underarm: 'I am such a bad sleeper.'

Remember, these are just suggestions to get your own ideas stimulated. What is right for you is what is relevant for you.

THINK ABOUT IT Once you're in bed and trying to sleep, most people find that it is better to just imagine they are tapping, rather than to actually tap, or to tap the side of the hand point and then imagine they are tapping the rest of the points. If you have tapped, your unconscious mind will know what you mean and will do it for you.

This has three obvious advantages over actually tapping.

1. When you are trying to get to sleep you want to relax. You do not want to be physically active.

2. Often when we have trouble sleeping it is caused by or causes lots of busy thinking. If you tie up your thoughts with really imagining each point in turn, they have less capacity to run off in anxious directions.

3. If you are not sleeping alone, imagining tapping is less likely to disrupt your partner's sleep than actually tapping.

Nightmares

Some people are reluctant to go to sleep because they are afraid of having nightmares. If you think this may be you, tap on this fear. But it's also useful to look at nightmares as opportunities rather than ordeals. Let me explain why. We know that what we dream, whether it's horrific or bland, is something that our unconscious minds are trying to work out. The language of dreams is metaphor, and some people like to try to crack the code.

But with EFT, you can use dreams without ever working out what they are about. You can just tap on a dream in the same way as you would an actual memory. That way at least its negative emotional hangover will clear and at best your unconscious mind may be able to finish processing what-ever it was trying to process without your ever having to become aware what it was.

So just like a short actual memory, pretend you have a copy of it on a DVD, give it a title and rate on a scale of 1–10 how much the memory of the dream disturbs you. Then do the Movie Technique on it, as if it was something that had really happened to you.

 James had a recurring nightmare in which he was being chased by a tiger. Then there would come a point when he had the tiger by the throat and knew that if he let go, it would kill him. But he was finding it harder and harder to hold on ... He remembered he had had it since he was a small boy. Now he did not have it often. But once every couple of months, it would be back.

After he learned about EFT he did the Movie Technique on it. The emotional intensity went out of the memory of it. His recall of it seemed less vivid than it had been. A year later, he had still not had it again.

He never did discover what the dream was about. But he did not need to. EFT had somehow enabled his unconscious mind to finish the processing it had been trying over and over again to complete.

PART FOUR:
EFT for moving forward

---

24. Undoing trauma

EFT is amazing for dealing with trauma for two reasons. First, it has the ability to detach from the memory of the event the negative emotion that has been stored with it. And second, it has ways of doing it that have less risk of re-traumatizing us than any therapy technique before it. This is because most trauma techniques involve going back over the trauma and reliving it. For many people the reliving is potentially re-traumatizing.

EFT has ways of reducing the emotion about a traumatic memory *before* you go back to it in any detail. This chapter will explain how to do that. But how do you tell when a negative memory is actually a traumatic one? And how can EFT help if it is? Traumatic memories somehow get stuck in the system, like an undigested meal in your stomach. They may be of something that happened ten years ago but they feel as if they were recent.

The ordinarily-awful goes into long-term memory fairly quickly. Say someone takes your mobile phone. You might be angry with them. You might be angry with yourself. You might feel more vulnerable. You might be more anxious, even over-anxious, about where you keep valuables when you are out, for a time. You will probably go over it in your head and probably talk to friends about it for a while, and gradually you will have a 'story' about it. You'll get to a point where you wish it had not happened but you know it is not going to ruin the rest of your life. You'll move on.

But some events overwhelm our resources so we cannot do this. They get stuck in more short-term memory in a part of the brain with no real language facility. They continue to seem more recent than they actually were. Some or all of the relevant sensory information that goes with them – sight, sound, feeling, and even smell and taste – is stored rather than fading away.

Sometimes traumatic experiences are obvious and indisputable. If you're caught in a tsunami, trapped in a falling building in an earthquake, or if you see a comrade blown up in a war zone or survive a serious car crash, no-one would doubt that that was a trauma. Anything where the thought at the time is 'I am going to die' is an obvious trauma.

But there are also other, seemingly-smaller events that are what are sometimes referred to as 'small t traumas' because they are not obviously life-threatening but do have a lasting effect. They are more subtle. They are life-defining and life-changing, rather than life-threatening. They may be a point at which we make a decision or take on board a belief that changes us for the rest of our lives. We may not even know we did. They may not make us afraid that we are about to die. Nevertheless they, or their aftermath, stay in our systems until we do something to get rid of them. We may remember them. Or we may just accept, unchallenged, the new belief or direction we adopted at that time, even if we were very young.

IF YOU REMEMBER ONE THING Although EFT is a good way to deal with traumas and their aftermath, it is not advisable to work on your own with memories of early abuse whether it is sexual or emotional, or with any trauma or series of traumas that have left you with Post Traumatic Stress. If you are having nightmares or flashbacks or you cannot sleep because of intrusive memories, you really need to work with someone with expertise and who can give you support.

If you do start tapping on traumatic memories and find your symptoms are getting worse, or that tapping has taken your focus to a bigger trauma than you started on, keep tapping on the feelings that are coming up to keep yourself calm – and seek expert help. There is information on how to find qualified EFT practitioners at the back of this book.

Sometimes a factor in what makes seemingly small events traumatic is our age when they happen. The first day a parent takes a child to school and leaves him there can be traumatic for some children. Or another might be devastated when her mother comes home with a new baby.

Don't dismiss the seriousness of an early traumatic memory because to you now, as an adult, it seems trivial. You can only get a sense of how influential it has been by asking yourself how traumatic it would have been for someone of the age you were when it happened. EFT can deal with all those traumas from the 'small t trauma' to a major threat to survival – in much the same way.

When you are working on disempowering old negative memories, and you want to rate the SUDS – the 1–10 level of distress or disturbance – it is better not to distract yourself from the main agenda by giving attention to what emotion or emotions you are feeling. This is not the time to put them in a category. Just go for an overall level.

 The Movie Technique
Remember the Movie Technique in chapter 5? If you skipped it or missed it go back and have another look at it, as it is one of EFT's best workhorses. Master it and you will be amazed at what you can do to change how you experience your life from now on. The movie technique is fine if your memory is mild to moderate in the emotional response you have to it.

If a memory still has high emotional intensity, you do not even need to run your DVD before you have tapped to take some of the sting out of it. Instead of calibrating it by running it to discover how high your response is to it now, you just guess what the emotional intensity would be if you did. (This is the Tearless Trauma Technique that you first met in chapter 6.)

Storytelling

Just tapping repeatedly on a memory will get boring. So when you have got it down to a fairly low number, you can switch to storytelling. Or, if you struck lucky and it quickly went to zero, you can use this to test the result of your work. This is particularly useful for more serious trauma.

What you do is this: tell yourself the story of your trauma as if you're telling someone who has never heard it before, in as much detail as you can remember. Tell it out loud if you can. Every time you feel even a tiny bit of emotion, stop and tap on that emotion until it clears.

Back up a sentence and carry on until you hit the next emotion. When you can tell the story from beginning to end without feeling anything you are done. As you work through this stage and emotions come up it's useful to notice not only that an emotion has come up but what emotion it is. Is it fear? Or anger? Or anxiety? Or guilt? And where and how do you feel it in your body. Your 1–10 no longer needs to be a general level of distress or disturbance, as it was when you started tapping on the whole memory, but can instead be related to these specific feelings. If you tap on something like 'this burning red anger in the pit of my stomach', for example, you will get a better result and faster than if you are more vague about what you are experiencing.

THINK ABOUT IT

There is something about telling the story that often accesses details that you had completely forgotten. It will also bring out any lurking feelings that we have managed to hide from ourselves.

Aspects

Even a short specific memory like being in a car crash will often have a lot of specific aspects. So, for example, you might remember the moment you realized the lights of an oncoming car were not where they should be. Then you might remember the metal on metal sound of the crash. Then you might remember someone screaming. Then you might remember what a paramedic said to you as they got you out of the car. Each of these would have its own emotional peak and would need to be tapped in turn, as if each was a separate memory. The combination of telling the story and using EFT as each new aspect comes up can make all the difference.

CASE STUDY

Elena was a student who volunteered to work with me on the memory of a car crash some years earlier so I could demonstrate to the students how one specific short trauma can have many different relevant aspects.

176

The event had a number of them and we made a different specific movie of each of them and tapped on them one at a time. There was the glare of the approaching headlights. Then there was the crunch of metal. Then there was being cut out of the car. Then suddenly she had a revelation. She had completely forgotten the worst bit of it. There had been a time when she was trapped in the car and terrified that it would burst into flames and she would burn to death. That was obviously so terrifying that she had repressed it completely.

When we tapped on that newly-recovered memory the whole old event memory became emotionally neutral for her. It really was a thing of the past.

Staying even safer

There is no limit to how much you can distance yourself from a memory until you get it down to a more manageable emotional level. The more you do, the less danger there is that you will re-traumatize yourself.

So instead of imagining that you have a memory on a DVD on your 'memory shelf', you can imagine that you have it behind a heavy curtain, or in the next room, on a spaceship circling the earth, or on another planet. And remember that, wherever you have put it, if you know it is high intensity you should start with the Tearless Trauma Technique above before you move on to the Movie Technique.

25. Tapping into forgiveness

Many of us find forgiveness really difficult. If we forgive someone does it mean they got away with what they did to us? If we forgive ourselves does it mean we might just do the same wrong thing again? If we do not forgive does that mean we are somehow not as good as people who do? What if we really do not want to forgive? And how do you do it anyway?

There are so many different ways people define forgiveness. Here is mine:

By forgiving others, I mean cutting the negative energetic connection that keeps us linked to someone for as long as we decide not to forgive them. It does not mean that what they did is okay. If it was not, it is still not. It is just that we have decided not to stay connected by this negative energetic bond.

Sometimes people say: 'If I forgave them I would be letting them off the hook.' They say it not realizing that the person they are refusing to forgive forgot all about whatever it was they did years ago. This connection may, by now, be a one-way thing.

Forgiving others is a game of two halves. First we have to decide we are willing to. Then we have to find how.

Many studies have found that people who do not forgive have more stress-related illness, poorer immunity and worse rates of cardio-vascular disease than those who do. People who forgive have better heart function and better recovery if they do have a heart attack.

If you ask someone to think about the grudges they are still holding onto from the past their blood pressure immediately goes up and their heart rate increases. Letting go is good for us.

FORGIVENESS STRATEGIES

Even when you decide that you want to forgive someone in theory, emotions may still get in the way. And there might be some inner conflict. So one part of us might believe we really will be healthier and happier if we forgive someone while another part completely resists it.

Here are some of the things you might find you need or want to tap on to help get past those emotional blocks. Read them out loud to see which ones strike a chord with you, or which, when you hear them, throw up other ideas for you. Tap on what seems relevant, or even just might be.

'Even though I really don't want to forgive this ...'

'Even though I really don't want to let them off the hook ...'

'Even though I don't know how to forgive this ...'

'Even though they do not deserve to be forgiven …'

'Even though I don't know how to let this go …'

'Even though I'm not ready to forgive this …'

'Even though it's weak to forgive …'

Spontaneous forgiveness

One of EFT's strengths is that it can produce spontaneous forgiveness. Often, when we tap on old negative memories, as the emotion clears so does our view of the other people involved in the event we are tapping on. And the new view may be more forgiving, or may even be a recognition that no forgiveness is required at all.

So you might be tapping on a time you remember coming home from school and when you tried to tell your mother about it, she just brushed you aside. What made it worse for you was that this did not just happen once. It seemed to be happening all the time. You might be focussing on this memory because you feel it created and confirmed a belief that your mother did not love you.

As you peel away the emotional residue from the memory, you might suddenly realize: 'My mother was not being unloving to me. She was just so worried that the baby was ill and she had had almost no sleep and they were worried about how to keep up with the bills …'. The mother it was hard to forgive for not being a loving mother is suddenly transformed into a worried and stressed young woman struggling to cope with more pressure than she knew how to deal with. She no longer needs to be forgiven, just understood.

CASE STUDY Janice was at a workshop where she was learning EFT. She volunteered to tap in front of the group on her memory of a car accident twenty years earlier which had left her with a legacy of physical pain, especially in her left shoulder. Her range of movement had also been restricted ever since that day the car went off the road. Her other legacy of the accident was anger with the young driver who had been showing off by driving too fast.

As she worked on aspects of the accident, the pain went down and down. There was asking the driver to slow down and being ignored, and the moment she realized the car was going to go off the road, and the impact, and being pulled out by the ambulance crew. Finally, Janice realized there was just one piece of the emotion attached to the original memory left. She was still angry with the driver. She could never forgive him.

As she tapped on that anger, she found herself seeing him in a different way. He was young and showing off because he was so shy and unsure of himself. He did not realize how dangerous it was. As Janice found herself forgiving him without even trying to, she felt the last of her pain just drain away. And, when she gently tested it, she found the range of movement in her damaged shoulder had increased. It continued to increase over the next few days.

Twenty years of anger had gone – and the aftermath with it.

Forgiving ourselves

Many of us find forgiving ourselves even harder than forgiving others. It may be we don't think we deserve it. Or because we think if we do we could not trust ourselves not to do the same thing again. Or that we have not yet been punished for long enough.

MORE EFT STRATEGIES

Here are some of the thoughts that may be getting in the way. Tap on the ones you recognize or suspect are lurking in there unrecognized, and any others that come up for you as you do.

'Even though if I forgave I might not be able to keep myself safe ...'

'Even though it's weak to forgive ...'

'Even though I don't deserve to be forgiven ...'

'Even though I can never forgive myself ...'

'Even though I don't know who I would be without this guilt ...'

'Even though I could not trust myself if I forgave myself ...'

'Even though I am sure that the feelings will keep coming back ...'

Remember that this is just a sample of the blocking beliefs you may have to clear before you can forgive. None of them might hit the spot for you. But the great thing about EFT is this knack it has of taking us where we need to go. So if you have no ideas yourself and nothing here seems relevant for you start with them anyway and see where they take you.

 Just one thing – if you have not forgiven your-self for something you did and for which you know you could and should still make amends, think about making amends, too. Tapping is not meant to be a 'get out of jail free' card. It does not give us a licence to behave any way we like without consequences. You will find that the combination of making what amends we can and tapping to facilitate and consolidate self-forgiveness can bring a very deep level of inner peace.

26. Dealing with grief

When you lose someone close to you, it's inevitable that you will experience grief. The loss will continue to be a loss for the rest of your life. EFT cannot change that. But tapping can really help to manage the disorientating and shifting kaleidoscope of emotions – or lack of emotions – that may batter you or freeze you – as you find your way to come to terms with it.

Let's get one thing straight. There is no standard or right or normal way to experience grief, nor is there a standard or acceptable time frame. You may be plunged into deep despair by the death of someone close to you or be so numb you feel nothing. What you feel today may be nothing like what you feel tomorrow. Emotions can swing dramatically from morning to afternoon of the same day. You may think you have put your loss behind you just to find a new wave of emotions ambushing you again.

For generations conventional therapies have believed that:

a) when we grieve we will go through the stages of denial, anger, bargaining, and depression and that we will cycle backwards and forwards between them, before we get to acceptance.

b) it is a natural part of human nature, and that we should let these feelings run their course without interfering with them or we will be sorry later. We will be harmed in some way by the interference. Repressed emotions may still ride with us, or we may be stalked by emotions we can make no sense of.

But, despite the way this model of grief has seeped into our culture, there is no evidence for it. It has never been tested. Recent evidence seems to contradict rather than confirm it. So we can use EFT to help us through grief and its symptoms when we feel that we would like to, without fearing that we may be alleviating present distress at the risk of a future backlash.

THINK ABOUT IT Sometimes people are afraid to tap on memories of or feelings about someone who has died because they believe that if they do they will somehow erase their memory of or cut their remaining link with the person.

The reverse is actually true. When we clear negative emotions we do not lose the memory of the person. We often connect more strongly with positive memories, and with a reinforced positive link.

GRIEF STRATEGIES

First clear the trauma

Death is a natural part of life. But the manner of death, or of learning about it, or hearing a terminal diagnosis can be traumatic. And when it is, it can be hard to get past the trauma and back to connecting with the person we have lost as we knew them and related to them before the trauma.

- Do the Movie Technique on any negative memory you have of diagnosis, prognosis, being told about the person's death, or of how the person died.

- Do not limit what you categorize as a traumatic memory. A traumatic memory can arise from something we experienced and remember but it can equally arise from something we imagined. What matters is what is stored in our heads. A traumatic memory can be just as potent if we imagined we experienced it – or even more so.

 Jane and Ella had been good friends. They had always supported one another. So when Ella was terminally ill in hospital and Jane realized that she had no local family to visit her, she spent many hours at Ella's bedside. Ella was weak and very sick, and nothing could be done to alleviate her suffering. After Ella died, Jane found she could not really remember her as she had been in the long years of their friendship.

Whenever she thought of her, her memory was haunted by a picture of Ella emaciated, weak and in pain.

Jane did the Movie Technique on a couple of typical memories from that time. It was hard to know what was a single memory and what was a composite, but she knew that the historical truth did not matter. What was relevant here was what was stored in her head. When she cleared the hospital trauma memories, that stuck picture cleared from her head. She could remember Ella as she had been, the warmth of their friendship, the good times they had had together.

Challenge beliefs

Check out whether you have any negative beliefs about grief. Do you believe that it is 'normal' to take two years to get back to some kind of even keel after someone close to you dies?

Do you believe that it's not 'normal' if you do not let yourself suffer whatever grief throws at you? That it is OK to accept support but not OK to do anything that might change your feelings? Or do you think that if you reduce your own suffering you are somehow not respecting the person you have lost? Do you think you need to honour the memory of the person you have lost by suffering? Do you fear that you will forget someone sooner if you work on your grief?

You can tap on any beliefs you have that you know logically will make it more difficult for you to move on. Just check out how strongly that belief *feels* true, on a scale of

1–10, then tap on it. For example, 'Even though I have this belief [specify] I accept myself anyway.' Modify the wording as you work through it, for example, 'Even though I still have some of this belief …'. Rate the intensity again.

Reduce negative feelings

Just tap on whatever it is you're feeling. Do it without judging yourself, or evaluating how appropriate your feelings are, or censoring yourself in any way. Your feelings are what they are.

EFT can be particularly useful to help you get through things like funerals, if, for example, you are worried that you will cry or fall apart, and it's important to you that you don't in that particular circumstance.

Here are some examples of set-up phrases that will be relevant for some people. Just use them as a prompt to recognize and express your own.

'Even though I feel so flat today …'

'Even though I feel numb and dead …'

'Even though I feel so angry with them for dying and leaving me …'

'Even though I don't know how to pick up the pieces and go on …'

'Even though I feel so down …'

'Even though I am raging …'

'Even though I should be over this by now ...'

'Even though I feel OK today so I think there must be something wrong with me ...'

'Even though people are avoiding me because they don't know what to say ...'

'Even though I am hurt that people are avoiding me ...'

'Even though my friends don't want to hear me going on and on ...'

'Even though I thought I was okay and I seem to have gone backwards again ...'

'Even though I cannot stop crying ...'

'Even though I cannot cry ...'

'Even though we had that row and did not make up ...'

'Even though I did that to her ...'

When you tap on thoughts and feelings like these, it is important to really emphasize to yourself accepting yourself. You might like to use a variation like 'I accept myself anyway', or 'I accept myself without judgement' or 'I accept myself with compassion'.

EFT cannot abolish grief, and deep loss will always leave a sadness in your life. But tapping can be a useful ally when you want to minimize your suffering, and can help you get back into your 'normal' life when you feel ready to move on.

27. Attracting abundance with EFT

Abundance means plenty. It could mean an abundance of health, wealth, opportunities, relationships, the chance to develop our talents or spiritual growth – whatever you want it to be. But if you're looking for a get-rich-quick guide, this is not it.

The Law of Attraction describes the way that like attracts like, and that includes thoughts. If you think that your life is drudgery and a struggle, and bad things keep happening to you, then guess what? It's unlikely that things will change. But if you set the intention that your life will change, then changing the frequency of your thoughts in that way will start to attract different opportunities to you.

Whether you realize it or not, your current thoughts are creating the life that you are about to have. What you most think about or focus on will turn up in your life. As EFT Founder Gary Craig says: 'Your constant thoughts become your reality.'

Sound easy? There is just one drawback, but luckily this is exactly where EFT can help.

Let's say you really want to start your own business. You have an idea that you know could fly. You have researched the market. You have checked out what competition you would have. You have done the sums and know what it would cost and that you could sell it at a profit. You are all systems go to launch. That is what you think *consciously*.

But, at an *unconscious* level, you're running this conflicting scenario: 'Whatever I do, this will not work out because every time anyone in my family tries to go into business, they fail.' Or maybe it is: 'Whatever I do, this will not work because every time I try anything I end up failing again.'

So at a conscious level you may be sending the universe a shopping list for everything you need to succeed but unconsciously you are cancelling it out with exactly the opposite message.

 For as long as you have an unconscious negative belief that contradicts what you consciously think you want, it will cancel out whatever you have set as your intention to achieve.

ABUNDANCE STRATEGIES

EFT's contribution towards filling your life with abundance is to clear out the negative, blocking beliefs that you have whether you are consciously aware of them or not. Your job is to identify what they might be.

- **Start with the ones you know.** What is your previous experience of disappointment or even failure? Think back over things that have happened that made you feel a failure, or that you had not been chosen, or that good things only happen to other people. They do not have to be in categories in any way related to what you are trying to achieve now. Being picked last for a sports team, or even not being picked at all, could give you a message that will last a lifetime if you do not actively challenge it. Tapping on the memory of that event would be one way to do that. Tap, too, on the feelings you have about it.

- **Then guess the blocking beliefs you do not know.** What is your family's history of success or failure in the area in which you're seeking abundance? Do you have a belief that whatever negative family history you have will inevitably repeat itself with you? Even if you do not think you have, might you, deep down?

  Tap on the possibility. You can use words like 'Even though it is possible that a part of me thinks …'

- **Think of messages you got as a child** like 'You will never amount to anything', or 'don't do anything to attract attention'.

Sometimes parents or teachers brainwash us into having low or no expectations for all sorts of reasons that may not even be anything to do with us. They may be projecting their own disappointment with life on to us. Or they may be trying to protect us from disappointment. Or they may have a belief that 'if you keep your head down, you will be safer in life'.

Tap on these beliefs, or if you do not recognize them as part of the way you see the world, tap on something like 'Even though my mother told me ...'

- **Clear the decks.** There are many negative emotions that guarantee that our state of mind is incompatible with attracting all the good things that we want in our lives. They include fear, anger, helplessness, powerlessness, jealousy, envy, resentment. If you recognize that you are feeling any of these tap on them.

- **Raise your level.** Once you have cleared the drains on your vibrational level you can raise it even higher by increasing the amount of gratitude and compassion and love in your life. Do a gratitude list regularly. Walk in the park or in the countryside and notice all the things there are to be grateful for. Remind yourself of all the good things about yourself.

John was trying to set up a practice as a sports massage therapist. He had a good location in a thriving health centre. He had done really well on his training course and left with excellent qualifications and recommendations from his tutor. He had made all the right marketing moves.

But somehow, it was not happening. Other practitioners in the health centre were really busy. His practice was just a trickle. So why wasn't he getting a flow?

John was tapping on his feelings about his 'failure' when he suddenly remembered an incident when he was about five or six years old. He was at a children's party. He was really excited, and he ate too much. The combination of excitement and food really upset his stomach. He vomited on the carpet, in front of all the other children. His mother was embarrassed. The mother of the birthday boy was angry. Both told him he had been too greedy. He had had more than his share and now look what had happened …

Young John made a vow never to be greedy again. Somehow that translated into never having much of anything. That even included clients, though he did not realize it.

When he tapped on that incident with the Movie Technique and disempowered its emotional hold over his unconscious mind, his practice began to build.

---

28. Troubleshooting and moving forward

Now you've learnt the techniques and theories of EFT, the best thing you can do is practise. With time, it should become increasingly natural to you, and work quickly and effectively to rid you of negativity. But we all encounter bumps along the road, so if at any stage EFT seems not to be working for you, ask yourself the following questions:

- Are you being specific enough?

   EFT is at its best when we are being specific – specific emotions, specific events, specific angles of a problem, even specific problems.

- Have you addressed all the different aspects?

- Are you being persistent enough?

   Sometimes we just have to hang in there for a lot longer than we would like.

- Do you have unrealistic expectations? EFT is rarely a one-shot wonder.

- Have you switched aspects without realizing it? For example, if you're tapping on your feelings about your partner leaving you, have you switched to your partner trying to stop your child from seeing you? You probably need to deal with both, but one at a time.

- Have you jumped to a different emotion? Sometimes we think the level of emotion has not gone down because it has, but a different emotion has come up, and we do not notice that that's what has happened.

- Do you have a blocking belief you need to deal with first, such as 'EFT won't work for me' or 'I don't think I can ever get over this'?

- Are you letting your attention wander from what you're doing? Sometimes splitting off is a good short-term coping strategy but we cannot do therapy on ourselves if we are not present.

- Who would you be without this problem? Do you have fears about the answer to that question? If so, you need to deal with them first.

- How would you be without this problem? Do you have fears about the answer to that question that you need to deal with first?

- Check how you are wording the set-up. Is it really hitting the spot?

- Have you cleaned the words up? Remember always to tell it as it is. Your unconscious mind will not recognize what you are talking about if you do not use the language you have in your head.

- Are you tapping as if you mean it?

- Are you saying the set-up as if you mean it?

Sometimes the problem is that we have a conflict between different parts of ourselves. One part of us wants an outcome but another doesn't, and blocks us from achieving it. When there is a parts conflict like that, we can tap on set-ups such as:

'Even though it is possible that a part of me doesn't want to get over this …'

'Even though it is possible that a part of me doesn't think I deserve to get over this …'

'Even though it is possible that a part of me is afraid to get over this …'

'Even though it is possible that a part of me would not feel safe if I got over this …'

Add in anything you know or suspect or guess is true for you. Remember, you're only saying it is possible, not that it is true. So it doesn't matter if it is not relevant for you. It's quite safe to cover all possible bases this way.

I hope by now you will already have a sense of how you can transform your life with EFT. Or, even better, that you may already be transforming it. I know some people will have read the book straight through first, and may now be ready to begin to try it out, while others will have dived in and started doing it right from the off. There is no right or wrong way. Just your way.

However you have used it, I hope you will find that the early part of the book has given you a sense of what EFT is and where it comes from and the mechanics of how to use it, and that later chapters have given you a lot of detailed ideas about how you can use it for particular problems. As you continue to use EFT in your life you can come back to the book at any time, either for a reminder of how to work on these specific topics, or for a more general overview.

Whichever group you belong to, I would like to leave you with a final tapping suggestion. Whatever you are working on, this is a nice phrase to throw in: 'Even if I never get over this problem, I accept myself anyway.' Sometimes what we resist, persists. Just being a bit more relaxed about it and accepting of ourselves warts and all, as a work in progress, can make all the difference.

Appendix A

The Movie Technique

Throughout this book I have suggested using the Movie Technique for negative memories. So here, for easy reference, is a summary of what it is:

The Movie Technique is:

- suitable for short memories with a single emotional peak

- suitable for memories which, on a scale of 1–10 don't go past about a seven.

Imagine that you have this short event on a DVD. Give it a title so you can tell it apart from other memories. Run the DVD and find, on a scale of 1–10, how high your emotional response is to it NOW. You are not trying to remember what it was then. It is what is in your head now that matters.

Tap on the side of the hand point while saying three times the set-up: 'Even though I have this [name of DVD] memory, I deeply and completely accept myself.' Tap around all the other points using as the reminder phrase the DVD title.

Run the DVD again to access how much feeling is still attached. If it has gone down but is not yet zero, do another round with something like: 'Even though I still have some of this …'.

Check again. If it is now low or zero, tell yourself the story, out loud if you can, and see if any emotion comes up as you tell it. If it does, stop and tap until that emotion has gone. Then back up and resume telling. When you can tell the story from start to finish without feeling any emotion, you are done.

The Tearless Trauma Technique

- is suitable for short memories with a single emotional peak of really high intensity, say eight or more.

The only difference between this and the Movie Technique above is that, at the start, you do <u>not</u> run the DVD of the memory. You just guess how high the emotional distress would be if you did. Then you tap in the same way as above. When you want to access the intensity level again, you guess again.

When you are guessing a moderate level, you switch to the Movie Technique to continue.

Appendix B: FAQs

Does it matter which hand I use or which side of the body I tap?

No. Use either hand, and tap either side. And you do not need to worry about doing both sides. Just doing one is all that you need.

Can EFT make me feel worse?

Yes, and no. EFT will not make you worse. But it may make you **feel** worse in the short-term.

Sometimes this will be because you have repressed emotion about something and tapping may lift the repression so that you actually experience that feeling. When that happens, hang in there. This is an opportunity, if you keep tapping, to clear the emotion that was in your system but out of your awareness. Now it's available to deal with.

And sometimes you feel worse because EFT has an uncanny ability to track where you need to go. You may be tapping on one thing and another thing that you did not realize was connected pops up. This is also a great opportunity, not a contra-indication.

Why does EFT concentrate on the negative?

It does seem counter-intuitive when there is so much emphasis everywhere on positive thinking. But EFT focusses on negatives in order to bring up in the body the energy disruption associated with the negative, to make it available to deal with it. You want it present to tap on it.

If you think of editing a document, you would need to open the document first in order to edit it. Then you would save it when you had made the changes. That is just what EFT is doing.

Can I tap on a positive statement of what I want instead of a negative one?

You can. It will not do any harm. But it is unlikely to be as effective in the long-term as tapping on negatives. It is a bit like putting a plaster over a wound before you have cleaned it properly. You might feel better in the short-term but, unlike when you clear negatives out of your system, it is unlikely to last. At best, it is a short-term fix.

Of course the second part of the set-up statement: 'I accept myself' is positive. And this combination of acknowledging our problem but still accepting ourselves seems to be able to reduce our resistance to allowing EFT to change how we feel.

What do I do when I am somewhere that I cannot tap?

There are a range of options. For example, you can just tap the side of the hand point or the gamut point, or you can just imagine that you are tapping. If you have been doing it, your unconscious mind will know what it is that you are imagining.

People say EFT is a one-shot wonder. Is it?

EFT rarely clears a problem in one single session, despite what you may have read. Sometimes, if something is quite straightforward, it may be possible to clear it quickly and cleanly in a short time. More often we need to be prepared to persist.

How do I know the right words to say?

There are no 'right' words. The words that will work best for you are the words that describe, as honestly and in as much detail as you can, what you feel and how you feel it. So 'this heavy, dull dread in the pit of my stomach' is likely to get you a lot further than 'this anxiety'. Describe what you feel emotionally and physiologically. Don't try to fool yourself with a cleaned up version of what you *really* feel.

Remember the words themselves are not magic. Their role is just to keep your attention on what you are dealing with.

Do I have to say the words out loud?

The ideal is to say the words aloud, as if you really mean them. But in the real world, you just go for the best you can get. If that means doing it silently, you will probably find you get a good result anyway. Just make sure your attention stays on what it is you want to deal with. That is what the words are for.

How long will it take me?

This is the piece of string question. You never know when you start tapping on something whether it will be really straightforward, or whether it will turn out to be connected to other things you need to clear as well. The good news is that EFT will usually show you where you need to go. If you are tapping on one thing and another pops into your head, trust the process and go with what popped up.

How often do I need to tap?

If you decide to be your own EFT therapist, you need to make regular appointments with yourself to do the work. Regular doesn't necessarily mean frequent. You have to work out what you can comfortably fit into your schedule. After that, you can just tap as often as something is bothering you. It is a bit like apples and doctors – a bit of tapping a day keeps a lot of stress away.

I tapped and seemed to have got rid of a problem but it came back. Didn't it work?

Probably it worked on what you cleared but there is more work to do. Maybe you cleared some parts of the problem but there is another or are others that you did not deal with. Has the same part of the problem come back or a different one you did not tackle? Has the same feeling come back or is it a different one? Maybe what you tapped on is leading you to where you need to go next to find a more core issue?

And there are some things we do need to keep coming back to and tapping for again. Some physical ones, for example, need to be constantly 'adjusted'. If you brushed your teeth would you expect not to have to do them again tomorrow? In the same way some physical conditions will keep going back to a default setting unless you tap repeatedly to change it.

Can I use EFT on anything?

For yourself, you can try it on anything. But remember that it is not necessarily a substitute for conventional treatment of, for example, medical conditions and does not claim to be. If you have pain remember that pain is a signal and may be telling you that something really needs to be checked out.

Serious psychiatric problems are a contra-indication, unless you really know enough about them. If you are not a psychiatrist or a clinical psychologist, you may not know if you're removing what you thought was a negative symptom but was actually some kind of defence against something worse. You may remove it and end up in a worse place.

How can I get my partner/son/daughter/father/mother/boss/best friend to tap?

You can't, but you can tap on your own feelings about whatever it is that you would like them to tap on. Sometimes that makes more difference to them – as well as to you – than you might imagine. When you feel differently and interact with them differently sometimes things change because the dynamic has changed. You can only really work to change yourself, not others.

How do I tap on a memory when I am not sure if I really remember it?

It doesn't matter what really happened. And it doesn't matter if what you remember is second hand, i.e. constructed from what others have told you or even if you have imagined it. It is what is stored in your head that counts. Many people have been traumatized by imagining things that did not happen to them at all.

How can I learn more about EFT?

There are a multitude of resources available. You can see details of the courses by accredited trainers round the world on www.EFTInternational.org. The courses are for people who just want to learn to use EFT for themselves and for those who want to go on to qualify to use it as practitioners to use it with other people or, eventually to become trainers themselves.

Appendix C:
EFT training and resources

Judy Byrne can be contacted via her website www.eft judybyrne.website where you will also find free resources and up-to-date EFT news and can sign up for her newsletter.

To find other EFT Masters go to www.eftmasters.co.uk

To find EFT practitioners and trainers worldwide go to www.EFTInternational.org. The site has a free newsletter sign-up and has a summary of research into the efficacy of EFT.

Other useful sources of help:

Your GP surgery may have a practice counsellor to whom they may refer you.

The EMDR International Association, where you can find qualified EFT therapists: www.emdria.org

Mind, the mental health charity: www.mind.org.uk

Women's Aid, for victims of domestic abuse www.womensaid.org.uk

Victim support, for victims of crime: www.victimsupport.org.uk

Cruse for bereavement counselling: www.cruse.org.uk

Rape Crisis, for both recent and historic victims of rape: www.rapecrisis.org.uk

Childline, which offers telephone support for children: www.childline.org.uk

Silverline, which offers telephone support for older people: www.thesilverline.org.uk

Index